I0021157

Getting Started with hapi.js

Build well-structured, testable applications and APIs using hapi.js

John Brett

PUBLISHING

BIRMINGHAM - MUMBAI

Getting Started with hapi.js

Copyright © 2016 Packt Publishing

All rights reserved. No part of this book may be reproduced, stored in a retrieval system, or transmitted in any form or by any means, without the prior written permission of the publisher, except in the case of brief quotations embedded in critical articles or reviews.

Every effort has been made in the preparation of this book to ensure the accuracy of the information presented. However, the information contained in this book is sold without warranty, either express or implied. Neither the author, nor Packt Publishing, and its dealers and distributors will be held liable for any damages caused or alleged to be caused directly or indirectly by this book.

Packt Publishing has endeavored to provide trademark information about all of the companies and products mentioned in this book by the appropriate use of capitals. However, Packt Publishing cannot guarantee the accuracy of this information.

First published: April 2016

Production reference: 1060416

Published by Packt Publishing Ltd.
Livery Place
35 Livery Street
Birmingham B3 2PB, UK.

ISBN 978-1-78588-818-2

www.packtpub.com

Credits

Author
John Brett

Reviewer
Jan Lehnardt

Acquisition Editor
Reshma Raman

Content Development Editor
Mehvash Fatima

Technical Editor
Dhiraj Chandanshive

Copy Editor
Sonia Mathur

Project Coordinator
Kinjal Bari

Proofreader
Safis Editing

Indexer
Tejal Daruwale Soni

Production Coordinator
Melwyn Dsa

Cover Work
Melwyn Dsa

Foreword

hapi is a toolkit for web applications (and other HTTP servers) built by people with twice my experience and at least 10 times the smarts. They got the right team together and managed to work with the freedom to get it right this one last time—and they delivered.

hapi is also built by people who understand how to create, foster, and maintain a healthy and inclusive open source community, manage a responsible yet speedy release process, and be all around lovely people. If you are an end user or want to start contributing to the hapi ecosystem, you'll have great fun on your way with the clever technology and, even more so, with the great people.

From the first examples in the first chapter that you work through on your own to a fullfledged system that a large team can work on productively without stepping on each other's toes, *Getting Started with hapi.js* takes you on the journey to master everything you need to build everything from a hobby project to the most popular site on the Web.

The third step of my "usual process" of working with hapi is this: loving hapi even more.

I know you will, too.

Jan Lehnardt
CEO, neighbourhood.ie

About the Author

John Brett is a software engineer passionate about new technologies, open source, and building useful software while travelling the world. Starting out in Ireland with a degree in Computer Science and Software Engineer, he went on to join IBM through their premier internship Extreme Blue, later working on collaboration software as part of IBM's Software Group. There, John mainly worked with PHP and JavaScript, only working with Node.js in his spare time.

Later in his career, John moved to a growing SAAS company called D4H Technologies. As a lead engineer there, he developed tools to aid emergency response teams globally, all from a lighthouse in Dublin, Ireland. Here, John got more exposure to Node.js, leading D4H's first venture into Node using hapi.js, later joining the hapi.js core team

About the Reviewer

Jan Lehnardt is a developer and business person from Berlin, Germany. He is the Vice President of Apache CouchDB (`http://couchdb.apache.org`), the database that syncs at the Apache Software Foundation, and a co-inventor of Hoodie (`http://hood.ie`), the web app framework for frontend developers. Jan is the cofounder and CEO of Neighbourhoodie Software, a product and support company based on Hoodie, CouchDB, and general web-nerdery in Berlin. They are also behind `http://greenkeeper.io`, a service that sends you a pull request when any of your npm dependencies get an update. In his spare time, Jan co-organises JSConf EU, Europe's favorite JavaScript conference.

www.PacktPub.com

eBooks, discount offers, and more

Did you know that Packt offers eBook versions of every book published, with PDF and ePub files available? You can upgrade to the eBook version at www.PacktPub. com and as a print book customer, you are entitled to a discount on the eBook copy. Get in touch with us at customercare@packtpub.com for more details.

At www.PacktPub.com, you can also read a collection of free technical articles, sign up for a range of free newsletters and receive exclusive discounts and offers on Packt books and eBooks.

https://www2.packtpub.com/books/subscription/packtlib

Do you need instant solutions to your IT questions? PacktLib is Packt's online digital book library. Here, you can search, access, and read Packt's entire library of books.

Why subscribe?

- Fully searchable across every book published by Packt
- Copy and paste, print, and bookmark content
- On demand and accessible via a web browser

Table of Contents

Preface

Node.js has become one of the most exciting development platforms in recent times. Combined with the largest package ecosystem in the world, npm, it has become a game changer in enabling higher developer productivity strides in improved application performance and a more enjoyable developer experience overall, which has lead to widespread industry adoption.

This book is focused on hapi.js, which is a rich Node.js framework for building applications and services with the goal of enriching the development experience further. It aims to increase your productivity by providing the tools you need when you want them and getting out of the away when you don't.

Developed by the talented team at Walmart Labs to handle the pressures of the Black Friday traffic, the busiest day of online retail on the calendar, it is proven at scale and has since seen wider adoption, participation, and collaboration from the wider community. Its growing adoption can be put down to how easy it is to use and get started with along with its proven stability.

The Node.js programming paradigm is quite different to other server-side technologies, and as such, it can be common for developers to get stuck on design and programming problems, such as dealing with the asynchronous nature of JavaScript and structuring an application as it grows. This is where hapi.js excels; it enables developers to focus on writing reusable business logic instead of losing time focusing on building application infrastructure without obscuring important implementation details.

While it was originally built as a framework focused toward the rapid development of RESTful APIs, thanks to its fantastic ecosystem, it has grown into a fully-fledged framework suited to building static file servers, websites, and web applications with excellent support for building real-time applications added more recently.

Due to the modular plugin approach it provides, it allows an easier collaboration between teams in larger enterprise environments as well as an easy point of integration for third-party libraries.

If you plan to use hapi.js in your next project, whether it be a side project, work project, or open source project, this book seeks to give you an excellent point at which to get started and solidify any knowledge you might have if you have used Node or hapi.js before.

What this book covers

Chapter 1, Introducing hapi.js, serves as an introduction to hapi.js and some prerequisite learning of Node.js. It explains what hapi.js is, who created it, why it needs to exist, and how to create a simple hapi.js server.

Chapter 2, Adding Functionality by Routing Requests, is the beginning of your journey of building applications with hapi.js. It will cover some basics, such as routing and building APIs, websites, and applications with hapi.js, and will also cover some differences in design compared to other Node.js-based frameworks.

Chapter 3, Structuring Your Codebase with Plugins, introduces the plugin API in hapi.js, which is one of its core features. It will walk you through how to simplify an application structure gracefully using plugins and also cover server orchestration using modules from the hapi.js ecosystem.

Chapter 4, Adding Tests and the Importance of 100% Code Coverage, explores the importance of adding tests to an application. It will introduce you to some of the testing tools available in the hapi.js ecosystem and also guide you toward getting 100% code coverage with your tests.

Chapter 5, Security Applications with Authentication and Authorization, takes a deep dive into how authentication works in hapi.js with practical examples of different authentication protocols, including social logins. It also demonstrates scopes and how to use them to add permission levels to your applications.

Chapter 6, The joi of Reusable Validation, deals with the topic of validation in applications using the joi validation library from the hapi.js ecosystem. It covers how to validate objects and route configurations and how to reuse this to generate documentation for applications.

Chapter 7, Making Your Application Production Ready, covers multiple topics to leave you ready to build your first application, such as integrating popular databases and adding caching and logging to applications to help scale an application as well as give it visibility when running in a production environment. It also covers a variety of other sources to continue learning more about hapi.js.

What you need for this book

To try out the examples shown in this book, you will need a working installation of Node.js version 4.x or greater, as well as npm. You will need to be somewhat familiar with the terminal in order to launch applications and install modules from npm. You will also need an editor to modify the code and a browser to view your applications running.

Who this book is for

This book is for a developer with some JavaScript knowledge, with or without Node.js experience, looking to build their first applications or even just learn more about a best-in-class framework to build APIs and applications: hapi.js.

Conventions

In this book, you will find a number of text styles that distinguish between different kinds of information. Here are some examples of these styles and an explanation of their meaning.

Code words in text, database table names, folder names, filenames, file extensions, pathnames, dummy URLs, user input, and Twitter handles are shown as follows: "This creates a directory called `hapi-hello`, and makes it the current directory."

A block of code is set as follows:

```
validate: {
  headers: true,
  params: {
    userId: Joi.string().min(4).max(40).required()
  },
  query: false
}
```

When we wish to draw your attention to a particular part of a code block, the relevant lines or items are set in bold:

```
validate: {
  headers: true,
  params: {
    userId: Joi.string().min(4).max(40).required()
  },
  query: false
}
```

Any command-line input or output is written as follows:

```
$ npm install hapi-swagger inert vision
```

New terms and **important words** are shown in bold. Words that you see on the screen, for example, in menus or dialog boxes, appear in the text like this: "If you navigate to this URL, you should have **Hello World** returned to you."

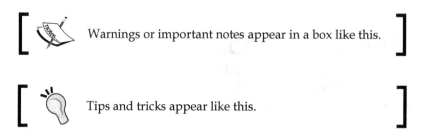

Warnings or important notes appear in a box like this.

Tips and tricks appear like this.

Reader feedback

Feedback from our readers is always welcome. Let us know what you think about this book—what you liked or disliked. Reader feedback is important for us as it helps us develop titles that you will really get the most out of.

To send us general feedback, simply e-mail feedback@packtpub.com, and mention the book's title in the subject of your message.

If there is a topic that you have expertise in and you are interested in either writing or contributing to a book, see our author guide at www.packtpub.com/authors.

Customer support

Now that you are the proud owner of a Packt book, we have a number of things to help you to get the most from your purchase.

Downloading the example code

You can download the example code files from your account at http://www.packtpub.com for all the Packt Publishing books you have purchased. If you purchased this book elsewhere, you can visit http://www.packtpub.com/support and register to have the files e-mailed directly to you.

Downloading the color images of this book

We also provide you with a PDF file that has color images of the screenshots/diagrams used in this book. The color images will help you better understand the changes in the output. You can download this file from `http://www.packtpub.com/sites/default/files/downloads/GettingStartedwithhapijs_ColorImages.pdf`.

Errata

Although we have taken every care to ensure the accuracy of our content, mistakes do happen. If you find a mistake in one of our books—maybe a mistake in the text or the code—we would be grateful if you could report this to us. By doing so, you can save other readers from frustration and help us improve subsequent versions of this book. If you find any errata, please report them by visiting `http://www.packtpub.com/submit-errata`, selecting your book, clicking on the **Errata Submission Form** link, and entering the details of your errata. Once your errata are verified, your submission will be accepted and the errata will be uploaded to our website or added to any list of existing errata under the Errata section of that title.

To view the previously submitted errata, go to `https://www.packtpub.com/books/content/support` and enter the name of the book in the search field. The required information will appear under the **Errata** section.

Piracy

Piracy of copyrighted material on the Internet is an ongoing problem across all media. At Packt, we take the protection of our copyright and licenses very seriously. If you come across any illegal copies of our works in any form on the Internet, please provide us with the location address or website name immediately so that we can pursue a remedy.

Please contact us at `copyright@packtpub.com` with a link to the suspected pirated material.

We appreciate your help in protecting our authors and our ability to bring you valuable content.

Questions

If you have a problem with any aspect of this book, you can contact us at `questions@packtpub.com`, and we will do our best to address the problem.

1
Introducing hapi.js

hapi.js (commonly referred to as **hapi**) stands for **HTTP API**. It is a rich framework for building applications and services. It was originally designed for the rapid development of RESTful API services using JavaScript, but has since grown to be a full web application framework with out-of-the-box features for templating, input validation, authentication, caching, and more recently, support for real-time applications with web socket support.

The original philosophy that hapi was built around was increasing developer hapi-ness; the aim was to increase productivity by providing additional tools to help with development, but without getting in the way. It was also built with a security-first approach, meaning that the tools provided were developed with smart secure defaults, with the mindset of not giving the developers the ability to shoot themselves in the foot for not knowing some hidden configuration setting or implied design pattern.

hapi was created by the Mobile team at Walmart Labs, led by Eran Hammer (who created OAuth), to handle their traffic for events like Black Friday, one of the busiest days for online shopping in the US calendar.

hapi was born out of necessity; the Walmart team never intended to build a framework. They originally started with express, currently Node's most widely used framework. After hitting some limitations with express, and finding similar limitations in other frameworks, they finally discovered that it would be easier to create their own framework rather than hack an existing framework to meet their needs. Eran wrote a great post about this journey on his blog, `http://hueniverse.com/2012/12/20/hapi-a-prologue`; I encourage you to read it. Fortunately for us, hapi was born out of all this.

This chapter will be your introduction to hapi.js, and will cover the following topics:

- Introducing Node.js—a prerequisite to learning hapi.js
- A background on hapi.js
- Creating our first hapi.js server

Node.js – a prerequisite to learning hapi.js

As this book is aimed at JavaScript developers, who may or may not have prior experience with Node.js (`https://nodejs.org/`), I would like to first introduce Node.js. Node.js (commonly referred to as **Node**) is a platform built on Chrome's JavaScript runtime called V8 for easily building fast and scalable web applications in JavaScript. To put it succinctly: server-side JavaScript.

The thought of server-side JavaScript might seem strange to those unfamiliar with the concept, but it has some big advantages over other server-side technologies such as PHP, Java, Ruby, and many others. For one, V8, on which Node is based, is fast, and has a full-time team in Google constantly improving its performance with each release of Chrome. One of Node's biggest differentiators as compared to other server-side technologies is its single-thread nature, encouraging the asynchronous coding style that you may be familiar with from working with JavaScript on the client side. Among its asynchronous nature, Node.js has many advantages, some of which are as follows:

- Reduces the need for multi-threading, always considered a tough problem in application development
- Allows sharing of code between browser and server, and avoiding a context switch between working with the browser and client
- It comes bundled with npm, currently the biggest package manager and one of the best solutions out there for managing your application dependencies on both client and server seriously, you will struggle to move back from Node after having the luxury of such an excellent resource

As a result of these and many other benefits of Node, many large organizations such as Netflix, Yahoo, Mozilla, PayPal, and of course the organization behind hapi.js, Walmart, have adopted Node. If you aren't familiar with Node or npm, I suggest you take some time to read up on them at `https://nodejs.org/about`, `https://docs.npmjs.com`. The Node.js website covers the installation of Node, and I suggest you do this so you can participate in this next part.

Let's take a look at what a simple' hello world' API server looks like in Node.js by using the example from the Node.js website (please take note that you need Node version 4 or greater to run this code, otherwise you will get syntax errors!):

```
const http = require('http');                            // [1]
const hostname = '127.0.0.1';
const port = 1337;
http.createServer((req, res) => {                        // [2]
  res.writeHead(200, { 'Content-Type': 'text/plain' }); // [3]
  res.end('Hello World\n');                              // [4]
}).listen(port, hostname, () => {                        // [5]
  console.log(`Server running at http://${hostname}:${port}/`);
});
```

You can download the example code files for this book from your account at http://www.packtpub.com. If you purchased this book elsewhere, you can visit http://www.packtpub.com/support and register to have the files e-mailed directly to you.

You can download the code files by following these steps:

- Log in or register to our website using your e-mail address and password.
- Hover the mouse pointer on the **SUPPORT** tab at the top.
- Click on **Code Downloads & Errata**.
- Enter the name of the book in the **Search** box.
- Select the book for which you're looking to download the code files.
- Choose from the drop-down menu where you purchased this book from.
- Click on **Code Download**.

Once the file is downloaded, please make sure that you unzip or extract the folder using the latest version of:

- WinRAR / 7-Zip for Windows
- Zipeg / iZip / UnRarX for Mac
- 7-Zip / PeaZip for Linux

I won't cover what happens here in detail, but will skim over the need to know parts to help understand how a typical Node server operates. With reference to the numbers in the code comments, let's go through each line:

- [1]: This is an example of using modules in Node.js. While many modules need to be downloaded using npm install, some modules like http are bundled with the Node binaries. In this example, we require the http module and assign it to the variable http. This is where we first see the ES6 syntax being introduced through the const keyword. Here, const basically specifies that we cannot redefine the http variable. If you want to read more about how Node modules work, you can find a good explanation in the Node API documentation at https://nodejs.org/api/modules.html.

- [2]: Here, we use the createServer method of the http module. We pass a callback function as an argument, which will then be called every time the server receives a request. This is the second example of the ES6 syntax being introduced, which is the arrow function. I suggest you read up on its differences with a normal function call at https://developer.mozilla.org/en/docs/Web/JavaScript/Reference/Functions/Arrow_functions. The callback function then takes two parameters: req, which contains information about the request that the server has received, and res, which is an object that contains the methods for responding to a request.

- [3]: Here we see the low level to which the Node http module goes, where you must set response headers and status codes; this is done by calling res.writeHead().

- [4]: The line res.end() signals to the server that all of the response headers and body have been sent, and the server should consider this request complete.

- [5]: Now that we have a server defined, we must tell it to accept connections for a particular port and hostname, and this is done by the server.listen() method.

That was a lot of information at once, so don't worry if it didn't make sense immediately; the concepts introduced here will become clearer as we talk more about them throughout this book.

To run this example, you should have Node installed. As I mentioned previously, instructions can be found on the Node.js website. Next, you need to create a folder and change to its directory:

```
$ mkdir hello-node && cd hello-node
```

Then create a file called `hello-node.js`, paste it in the preceding code and run it using the following command:

```
$ node hello-node.js
```

If all goes well, you will see the following screen:

Looking back at the preceding example, think now, how would you add functionality to this server while keeping your code base manageable? It certainly is not trivial. Especially when taking into account that typical servers will want to be able to serve static content as well as plaintext, JSON, XML and many other types. Often, it would need to deal with different request URLs and respond accordingly. Generally, it would need to interact with some type of persistent data store such as MySQL, and we still haven't even thought about authentication, authorization, validation of requests, and a number of other features that a typical application would need. This is what we refer to as application infrastructure, and this is where hapi.js comes in.

hapi is, in one sense, an abstraction layer on top of this low-level server, for providing more intuitive APIs for solving the previously mentioned problems, so you don't need to. It is a rich framework that allows you, the developer, to focus on writing reusable application logic instead of spending time building infrastructure.

The hapi philosophy versus other frameworks

Throughout Walmart's journey of rebuilding their mobile services tier and working with other frameworks, they realized that certain values were vital to building applications in Node for keeping the code intuitive, maintainable, and scalable. As a result, hapi centered around the following concepts:

- Time and effort should be spent on delivering value, not on rebuilding application infrastructure
- Configuration is better than code
- Business logic must be isolated from the transport layer
- Open Source and community-centric from day one

Let me elaborate more on hapi and these points, the thought process behind them, and how they compare to other frameworks in Node.

Building value, not infrastructure

As I mentioned at the start of this chapter, hapi aimed to be a solution for the rapid development of RESTful APIs, but has since grown to be a framework for handling other aspects of a fullstack web application like templating, caching, and more. To describe it best, hapi is a unified framework that aims to solve the common problems with building web applications with out-of-the-box functionality so that you don't have to.

There are competing strategies' frameworks use to provide a boost in productivity. Some take the "all-in" and highly opinionated approach by providing large amounts of frameworks features, APIs, and code-generation tooling. Loopback (`http://loopback.io/`) by Strongloop is an example of this in the Node world, or Rails (`http://rubyonrails.org/`) if you are familiar with Ruby. While this offers an initial productivity gain, I'm not a fan of this approach, as these frameworks usually have quite a large API surface area, which means that you spend a lot of time learning the framework API instead of learning JavaScript or whatever the underlying technology is. It also means that if the framework doesn't account for your particular needs, you have to hack against it, and when something goes wrong, you're left debugging generated or framework code which you're unfamiliar with. Experts in these types of frameworks can be very productive, but I generally prefer approaches that involve more exposure to application code and structure, as I find it's one of the best foundations in which to grow as a developer.

In contrast to the all-in framework approach, is the minimalist framework approach, which usually aims to act more as a user-friendly API. express on the server side or Zepto.js (`http://zeptojs.com/`, a lightweight jQuery alternative) are examples of these. There are lots of advantages of these kind of frameworks, as they remove a lot of boilerplate such as accounting for different runtime environments or browser differences, and usually have less performance overhead as the library size is small.

The downside to these frameworks is that, for larger apps, it is generally up to the developer to create their own framework on top of these to break up the business logic of the application into smaller, more loosely coupled, and manageable parts. This is one of the more complicated parts of building non-trivial applications. It also leads to spending time rebuilding common features of an application which generally don't add much business value, for example authentication. It was this desire to spend time on business value instead of building application infrastructure and common application features that made me research the available Node frameworks, and thankfully, I found hapi.

hapi treads the line quite nicely between being minimalist and providing too much tooling. Some of the out-of-the-box functionality I mentioned earlier covers areas like authentication, caching, validation, and of course, plugins. The hapi plugin system also provides the perfect abstraction for divvying up your business logic into manageable pieces. It also makes it trivial to avail of plugins from the hapi core team and the wider ecosystem to provide the building blocks you need. It encourages a great level at which to encapsulate the code in a structured and obvious manner. This makes hapi code bases usually much easier to maintain and comprehend due to their plugin-centric approach. I will cover plugins and the out-of-the-box functionality that hapi offers in detail in later chapters.

Configuration is better than code

One of hapi's code design principles is centered around the idea that configuration is better than code. This is one of the concepts I disagreed with before using hapi.js. I remember the nightmare of configuring development environments in Java and PHP, and I thought this is where Node.js excels — avoiding config problems! However, I've found application/framework configuration done well as an excellent approach for a number of reasons.

For one, when done with smart, secure defaults, it helps developers avoid making unnecessary mistakes. You shouldn't be punished for not knowing some configuration setting, or for some non-obvious convention. The thought process behind this is that it is easier to detect missing/wrong configuration than missing code. This gives hapi.js a huge advantage in that it provides much more detailed error messages for anything that is misconfigured.

You'll find so many more errors with detailed error messages on startup instead of at runtime. This speeds up the feedback loop on the effect your added/changed code has, which makes developing applications much more enjoyable and satisfying. A great example of this is in-route configuration. Any mistake here will be listed on server start, with line numbers and a detailed explanation of what is wrong, instead of trying to debug why handlers are not being called, or being called in the wrong order. These types of runtime errors often throw no error at all, and are quite difficult to debug.

Another example of this is limiting the file upload size by default. This means when you release your application to production, file uploads won't buffer an entire file into memory crashing your server. With hapi, by default, the max upload size is limited, and an error message will be returned to the user, making it clear that the file size is too large. You, the developer, then have the choice to increase this and learn about the pitfalls of buffering files into memory, while your application is up returning error messages, and not while your application is in production, being repeatedly brought down by large file uploads.

Separation of business logic from the transport layer

The hapi team encountered a number of issues in their early attempts to build their mobile tier at Walmart with other frameworks, a number of which stemmed from a mix of business logic with a transport layer. These issues ranged from trivial to complex.

In the preceding Node.js example, we've seen that we have to set headers, status codes, and specify the end of the response. While this is easy to follow in the preceding example, this quickly leads to unnecessarily complex code when returning more complicated structures. For example, if you swap out 'hello world' with a normal JavaScript object, the server now fails to return anything, and even worse, you won't discover this until you test how the server is responding to requests when running.

A more complicated example of this is routing collisions. In express and most other Node.js frameworks, routing is non-deterministic, which means that you can have two routes that will both be called for a particular URL path. This, like the preceding issue, is a more prevalent issue in larger applications where there may be different teams working on different parts of a bigger application. This can be quite hard to test for it is not an error, and can usually only be tested for at request time, much like the aforementioned issue. Furthermore, the order in which they are called is decided by the order in which they are registered.

This means that developers have to be careful when registering routes, or they may accidentally register a handler that is called twice, or expose a certain route before an authentication handler, for example, causing security issues. Routing conflicts may seem easy to spot, but when there are a large number of routes, and they can be defined using regular expressions as the routing patterns, this can happen more easily than you think.

To combat this, the hapi team designed a deterministic routing algorithm ensuring that there can be no conflicting routes. To aid productivity and developer happiness here, conflicting routes will fail on server start with the initial run, providing a detailed error message and thus making it simple to debug and fix.

They also created a reply interface that accepts objects, node streams, strings, promises, and buffers. This interface detects the data type, and acts accordingly so that you don't have to do extra work for the common, yet different response types.

Eliminating the possibility of conflicting routes, and reducing areas where you can have no error with no response via the reply interface are great examples of where hapi does its best to increase developer productivity by making it easier to catch common errors that can normally be difficult to spot.

Open source and community-centric

With hapi, you don't just get a framework, you also join a welcoming and inclusive community that wants to help you learn and succeed. You will find that most questions are asked through GitHub instead of the usual Stack Overflow, and are answered quite frequently by other members of the community as well as the core team. The entire time I have been working with hapi, I have been continually impressed by the community—from how it deals with and communicates breaking changes, encourages newcomers, and in how people respond to issues on GitHub. If you are working with hapi, don't neglect this as a resource.

Like most frameworks these days, hapi has been open source from day one, with a full-time team supporting it. This makes it a great learning resource, and I encourage you to read through the source code at times. Its style guide and talented contributors have created a code base with great examples of clean and well-structured code.

As a result of such great community support and involvement, the open source focus and hapi's excellent plugin system, a large ecosystem of quality plugins has been created for hapi too. A website has also been created to navigate these at `https://hapi-plugins.com/`.

The encouraging and inclusive nature of the community meant that my first npm module was a hapi module, my first conference talks were about hapi, I eventually become a lead maintainer of one of the core library modules, and am now writing a book (this!) to share the positive experiences that I've encountered in developing with hapi and being a part of its community.

Ecosystem

The hapi core ecosystem was the first of its kind (that I'm aware of) to only use modules that had 100% code coverage, strictly adhered to SemVer (`http://semver.org/`), a specification for communicating breaking changes, and only depended on modules that adhered to the same criteria.

If you're unfamiliar with SemVer, and it's something I also encourage you to read about, it stands for semantic versioning. It's a method of versioning modules that is easier for humans to read and understand (as opposed to machines), which communicates clearly breaking changes. When done properly, this means you can update the modules that your application depends on, availing of new features, performance improvements, bug fixes, and so on, without worrying about breaking your application.

In contrast, most modules/plugins for other frameworks are created by third-party users, and hugely vary in quality. Many have poor (or no) test coverage, and may cover only one particular use case. This leads to module discovery being a problem where the productivity increase of availing the existing modules is offset by having to take time to search, read the source, write your own tests, and debug issues of third-party modules.

Thankfully, the core hapi modules not only cover a wide range of functionality, but also have set a high standard for third-party modules; this has lead to an ecosystem of high-quality plugins for hapi. You can view the list of core modules within the hapi GitHub organization at `https://github.com/hapijs`.

Small modules

I often hear the argument of using only small modules to build applications in the Node community. With modules that do only one thing and do that one thing well, it makes it quite easy to use many of these to create full-featured applications easily. While this is appealing over learning the full API of a framework, it leads to the problem where the onus is now on the developer to decide on an application structure, write a lot of unnecessary code and infrastructure, and make a lot of unnecessary decisions.

The structure hapi provides, along with the use of configuration over code, leads to features and clever tools not possible with more minimal frameworks, or with the module-only approach. Examples of these are documentation generation tools like lout from the core team and hapi-swagger from Glenn Jones, which we will take a look at in later chapters.

Summarizing hapi

To summarize this section, hapi is a unified framework that aims to solve most problems that you encounter when building web applications as opposed to more minimalist frameworks that focus on providing more user-friendly APIs and utilities. It is building a lot of momentum and adoption in recent times, and you can check out the many companies using hapi on the hapijs.com community webpage at `http://hapijs.com/community`. But enough of the background—let's take a look at what a sample hapi.js server looks like in the next section.

Creating our first hapi.js server

I mentioned earlier in the chapter that I like to approach code and examples with a problem solving, code-first approach. So let's try that here. Our aim is to create an initial server that can respond to requests and will be our first experience with hapi. Let's see what it takes to install hapi and get our first hapi server running. I assume that by this stage, you have Node.js installed; if not, the Node.js website explains how to do this quite well. I also assume you have some experience with the command-line interface of your OS of choice. So to start our hapi.js project, first we'll create a folder within which we will create our server, Open your command line and type the following:

```
$ mkdir hapi-hello && cd hapi-hello
```

This creates a directory called `hapi-hello`, and makes it the current directory. Next we'll use npm to create our project metadata using `npm init`. If you installed Node successfully, the `npm` command will also have been added to your command line/terminal. One of the reasons to run this any time you start a node project is that any Node modules you install will be installed into this directory instead of its parent directory, as is the npm algorithm for installing modules. This also creates a `package.json` file in your current directory with all the metadata from the `npm init` command. You should take a look at this now.

Installing hapi

Next we will install the hapi module for use with this project:

```
$ npm install hapi --save
```

The `--save` flag tells npm to store this dependency in our `package.json` file. This is quite convenient for sharing this code with others, so we only need to share the actual application code and this `package.json` file. For another person to then run this project, they would just navigate to this directory and run `npm install`, and it would install all the dependencies listed in the `package.json` file. No messing around with the configuration of any kind.

Our first hapi server

With that, let's look at the code involved in our first hapi.js server:

```
const Hapi = require('hapi');                              // [1]
const server = new Hapi.Server();                          // [2]
server.connection({ port: 1337, host: '127.0.0.1' });      // [3]
server.route({                                             // [4]
  method: 'GET',                                           // [4]
```

```
    path: '/',                                          // [4]
    handler: function (request, reply) {                // [4]
      return reply('Hello World\n');                    // [4]
    }                                                   // [4]
});                                                     // [4]
server.start((err) => {                                 // [5]
  if(err) {                                             // [5]
    throw err;                                          // [5]
  }                                                     // [5]
  console.log(`Server running at ${server.info.uri}`);  // [5]
});                                                     // [5]
```

Again, I won't cover every detail here, but will give you the general gist of what's happening. Hopefully, you've noticed some similarities and differences between this example and the vanilla Node example given previously. With reference to the numbers in the code example, let's examine each section:

- [1]: We require the hapi module and store it in a variable Hapi, similar to importing the http module.

- [2]: We create a server with the hapi module, which is, in fact, the only function of the hapi module.

- [3]: Next we add a connection, which is a listener. We add the port and host configuration. This is quite similar to the listen function of the http server object, but here we configure it first, before we call listen or start our server. If no port is specified, a random port will be assigned.

- [4]: A sample route is added. This is slightly different to the preceding example, as it will only respond to 127.0.0.1 with Hello World and a 404 error to all other requests, whereas the preceding node example would respond to any URL. We can, of course, easily update this example to do the same, but I will cover that in the next chapter. This is where we see the configuration versus code approach more clearly—here we configure the route options as opposed to using code with a configuration object.

- [5]: Finally, we start the server that we have created. We also make sure to handle the error provided from the server.start() callback. This then ensures that all configuration is correct; if not, we want to throw the error so the server will not start and will send the error to the console, making it easy for us to debug.

What I hope is evident from the preceding example is that even though slightly more verbose, the hapi example is quite simple to follow and understand. All configuration is done when creating the server. Configuration is done when creating a route, which means well-defined handlers that can focus on just handling the request and not dealing with other parts of the transport layer.

To run this example, create a file in your current directory called `index.js`, and either type or copy-and-paste the preceding code. Then simply run the following command:

```
$ node index.js
```

If all goes as planned, you should see the following screen:

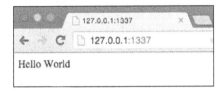

If you navigate to this URL, you should have **Hello World** returned to you. If all goes well, you will see the following screen:

Hopefully, you've been following the examples and creating this server yourself, so congratulations on building your first hapi server! Let's take a look at the configuration versus code here and see how it makes code easier to read, despite being a little more verbose. If you remember the `listen` method from our vanilla node example:

```
.listen(1337, '127.0.0.1')
```

You would have noticed that it uses parameters to pass in options such as `port` and `host`. In hapi, the equivalent is as follows:

```
.connection({ port: 1337, host: '127.0.0.1' })
```

This method takes a configuration object. This may not seem significant at the moment as these examples are quite trivial, but imagine when you have much more parameters which are Booleans, Integers, Strings, and so on—identifying what they are becomes a bit tougher. hapi is based around this concept of configuration objects making for much more readable code.

hapi plugins

Through its plugin API, hapi encourages a plugin-centric approach to development both, in the use of third party modules and also for your own features within your application. The plugin API makes it very easy to break an application into smaller plugins so that code is more manageable and readable. This is one of my favorite features of the framework, as it provides a convention for structuring your code in a scalable manner. We'll explore the plugin API in detail in *Chapter 3, Structuring Your Codebase with Plugins,* but I just want to introduce the concept, and show how to register a third party plugin here. Taking the preceding server example, it would be handy to have the server routing table display all routes on startup, and fortunately, there is a plugin for this called blipp.

If you explore hapi's plugins on the hapi plugin page, www.hapijs.com/plugins, you'll notice that a lot of the plugins have silly or non-descriptive names such as poop, joi, inert, h2o2, and so on. This is an attempt at creating competition for plugin implementation, for example joi; a model schema validation library could be named hapi-validator, but that would then be the standard validation library which doesn't encourage competition to build a competing schema validation library. The reason for silly names is an attempt to reduce the seriousness of enterprise development and make it more enjoyable for developers.

So let's look at an example of using a third-party plugin. Adding blipp to our example, we get the following code:

```
const Hapi = require('hapi');
const Blipp = require('blipp');                    // [1]
const server = new Hapi.Server();
server.connection({ port: 1337, host: '127.0.0.1' });
server.route({
  method: 'GET',
  path: '/',
  handler: function (request, reply) {
    return reply('Hello World\n');
  }
});
server.register(Blipp, (err) => {                  // [2]
  if(err) {                                        // [3]
    throw err;                                     // [3]
  }                                                // [3]
  server.start((err) => {
    if(err) {
      throw err;
    }
    console.log(`Server running at ${server.info.uri}`);
  });
});
```

With reference to the numbers in the comments in the preceding code example, let's examine each section now:

- [1]: We require the `blipp` module. Don't forget to install blipp through npm (`npm install blipp`) if you're trying this yourself.

- [2]: We register the plugin using `server.register()`. This is an asynchronous function. This is immensely useful for doing operations like initializing database connections on startup. An array of plugins can also be passed in here, which is also very useful for registering multiple plugins at once.

- [3]: We handle the error callback here. If there's any error, we will just throw it, and since it is uncaught, it will end the script execution and send the output to the console, again making it easier to debug what might have caused the error.

If you run this example, you will get the following output, which is the server routing table generated by the `blipp` module:

```
Johns-Home-Mac:example-3 johnbrett$ node index.js
http://127.0.0.1:1337
    GET    /

Server running at http://127.0.0.1:1337
```

Don't worry if this seems complicated now — we are just introducing the concept here. We will explore the `server.register()` API in depth along with creating your own plugins in *Chapter 3, Structuring Your Codebase with Plugins*; for now it is enough to know that it exists.

It's interesting to note that all of hapi was in 'core' at the beginning, in one repo. But over time, the hapi team broke out what functionality it could into plugins, making the hapi core project quite small, and each separate module much more manageable. All these plugins can be viewed in the hapi.js GitHub organization. They cover everything from payload and query string parsing to route matching, serving static content, and smaller utility modules like blipp in the preceding example. This approach is also very good when building an application — start with things in the core, and push functionality to plugins as the application begins to grow.

hapi configuration

hapi also has a concept of cascading configuration, which it's good to be aware of. That is, configuration of higher-level objects like the server and connection can be overwritten at lower layers such as plugins and routes, where the configuration is only applied at that level, much like how styles in CSS are applied.

A good example of how this is useful is authentication. Where we add and configure authentication, we would want to apply it to all routes within a server, and would do so at the server level. Then for one route to have no authentication required, for example a login page, we would just configure authentication to not be required on a particular route's configuration object. This may sound complex and tough to grasp initially, but as you see more examples of this, it will become clearer. It is enough just to be aware of it for now.

The hapi style guide

I'd like to draw your attention to the style of the code used in the preceding example. It adheres to the hapi style guidelines, and so will all examples in this book, as much as possible. I encourage you now to read the full list of rules on the hapi style guide available at `https://github.com/hapijs/contrib/blob/master/Style.md`. You may find that you have some disagreements with this and that's fine, but the importance of a style guide is not the individual rules, but that all the code is uniform. This makes spotting bugs and messy code much easier, and leads to clear code throughout the codebase. If you look at the hapi source code or source of hapi modules that adhere to the source, you will see a perfect example of this.

One aspect of the style I'd like to draw attention to is the functions versus fat arrow (=>) usage. If you look back to the previous example, you will see both are used, which might look inconsistent. The pattern used here is that inline callbacks must use arrow functions, while other functions may use either the arrow syntax or the function keyword. I currently use the `function` keyword anywhere I am not using an inline callback so as to support the use of the `this` keyword inside the `function` body.

So now that we know what a hapi server looks like, and what the code should look like in keeping with the style guide, let's take a look at how to add functionality to this application in the next chapter.

Summary

All code samples seen here as well as some extra material can be found online in the repository available at `https://github.com/johnbrett/Getting-Started-with-hapi.js`. If you have any questions about the code samples—in trying to understand code snippets or problems running them, feel free to open an issue.

In this chapter, we've introduced Node.js, its benefits and differences as compared to other server side technologies, and looked at what a simple Node.js server looks like. We looked at the reason for using a framework on top of this, mentioned some different frameworks, and introduced hapi.js as a choice. We talked at length as to why hapi.js is a good choice, who created it and why, and how its design principles differ from other Node.js frameworks.

Hopefully, at this stage, we've convinced you that hapi.js is a great choice for building web applications, and is something you want to learn about. Finally, we saw what a simple server looks like in hapi.js, using its style guide, and gave a quick overview of its excellent ecosystem and community. Next, let's look at adding functionality to our examples, and at creating a trivial applications and websites using the hapi.js framework and ecosystem.

2

Adding Functionality by Routing Requests

In the last chapter, we saw what a sample route looks like in both vanilla Node and hapi, and how hapi is more configuration-oriented in its routing definition. In this chapter, I will expand on how hapi handles routing, making it easy to add routes in a scalable manner while being able to avoid making unnecessary mistakes. If you haven't got much experience with building web servers, this chapter will also be a good foundation in routing, covering the following topics:

- Adding and configuring routes in hapi
- The hapi routing algorithm
- The hapi request life cycle
- The hapi request object
- The reply interface
- Serving static files
- Using templating engines to serve view

By the end of this chapter, you will have the tools that you need to be able to create a JSON API, a static file server, and a fully functional website using a templating library. You will also be shown some patterns to simplify less trivial requests, so the control flow won't become a problem while using the hapi life cycle and route prerequisites. That may seem like a lot to cover in a single chapter, but you'll find it's actually not so complicated, especially with the tools hapi gives us. Let's begin now.

Server routing

There are many ways to interpret a route in terms of web servers, but the easiest (or what I like to think of them as) one is the path that interacts with a particular resource on a web server. In most frameworks, including hapi, a route comprises three core properties:

- the path through which you can access the route
- a method by which you can access the path
- a handler, which is a function to take an action based on the request and return the output to the user

In hapi, the handler looks like the following:

```
...
server.route({
  method: 'GET',
  path: '/',
  handler: function (request, reply) {
    return reply('Hello!');
  }
});
...
```

The preceding code should look familiar to the code sample of our server from the previous chapter. Again, like everything in hapi, we add a route by providing a configuration object with the required route properties. If any required properties are missing, the server will show an error on startup with a detailed error message, thus making it very easy to debug routing configuration issues.

Route configuration

The example in the previous section was quite trivial; let's now look at a more detailed one, and examine the different parts of a route in hapi:

```
...
server.route({
  method: 'GET',                                          // [1]
  path: '/hello/{name}',                                  // [2]
  config: {
    description: 'Return an object with hello message',   // [3]
    validate: {                                           // [4]
      params: {                                           // [4]
        name: Joi.string().min(3).required()              // [4]
```

```
      }                                              // [4]
    },                                               // [4]
    pre: [],                                         // [5]
    handler: function (request, reply) {             // [6]
      const name = request.params.name;             // [6]
      return reply({ message: `Hello ${name}` });   // [6]
    },                                               // [6]
    cache: {                                         // [7]
      expiresIn: 3600000                             // [7]
    }                                                // [7]
  }
});
...
```

You will notice that the handler has moved inside the config object. When defining simple routes like our first one, this is not necessary. But as the route configuration becomes more complex, it allows us to simplify code by having the route controller logic in one object. This means that the logic could be defined somewhere else, like a different file, making for much easier management of code. This would be the 'controller' of the very common MVC pattern. With reference to the numbers in the preceding code example, let's now walk through our route configuration object:

Method

This is an HTTP request method defining how this route is to be accessed. It will generally be either GET, POST, PUT, DELETE, OPTIONS, or PATCH. A wildcard * can be used, but I've found this only to be useful for a catch-all route to return a '404 not found' message. A point to note here is that for GET and DELETE, a payload will not be parsed or validated, as they should only be supplied with a POST, PUT, or PATCH request.

Path

This is the address of the resource that you are accessing. Routes are split into segments by the / character, which can be accessed from request.params inside the route handler. Segments here can be any of the following:

- Required: /sample/{segment1}/{segment2}

  A request path must contain all segments to match this route.

- Optional (denoted by ?): /path/{segment1?}/something

  A request path must contain path followed by something, with an optional segment in between to match this route

- Wildcard (denoted by *): /path/{segments*}

  A request must contain a `path` segment, and then any number of segments from 0 upwards to match this route

- Limited wildcard (denoted by *limit): /path/{segments*2}

  A request must contain a `path` segment followed by up to two segments to match this route.

Do any of these routes conflict? Try to add all these examples, and see what happens.

Description

The description adds no functionality to the hapi server, but is a form of documentation for your routes and can be used in documentation generation tools like Blipp available at `https://github.com/danielb2/blipp` and Hapi-Swagger available at `https://github.com/glennjones/hapi-swagger`.

Validate

Using joi, an excellent model validation library also developed by the Walmart team, you can add route-specific validation here. This is quite a large topic, and will be covered in *Chapter 6, The joi of Reusable Validation*, but it's good to be aware of it now.

Pre

Pre is the object key for route prerequisites. Route prerequisites are an array of functions that are executed before the handler is invoked. This gives you the chance to abstract and remove any common functionality that you might perform in the handlers as well as set up database connections or perform any checks you might need. So, your handler can focus on responding to the original request, making for much more readable code. Functions can easily be executed in series or in parallel, making control flow much simpler.

A sample route prerequisite is of the following form:

```
const routePrequesite = { method: pre1, assign: 'm1' };
```

Here `pre1` is the function that will be invoked, and the optional assign key means that any value returned from the `routePrerequesite` will be stored in the `request` object, which will be accessible from:

```
request.pre.m1;
```

Let's look at what a full example would look like, noticing which prerequisites are executed sequentially and which in parallel (some route configuration code has been removed for brevity):

```
...
config: {
  pre: [
    setupDBConnection,                        // series
    checkUserExists,                          // series
    [ getUserDetails, getUserConnections ]    // parallel
  ],
  handler: function (request, reply) {
    const user = request.pre.userDetails;
    user.connections = request.pre.userConnections;
    return reply(user);
  }
}
...
```

See how much we can simplify handlers when route prerequisites are used?

Handler

The handler is likely where most of the action will happen, and where most of your time will be spent when adding routes while developing your web servers. I generally try to separate my logic so that the handler can focus on what the route is supposed to do, and push everything else to prerequisites, making for quite simple handlers. I will go through the request object and reply interface in more detail in later sections within this chapter, but for now it's enough to know the following:

- The request object contains all the data from the request, including the raw request along with the extra information provided in the earlier stages of the request life cycle.

- The reply interface returns whatever is provided to the user, and it will figure out the return type based on the data provided, such as JSON or PLAINTEXT. Also, one of the most common errors I see beginners make when starting out with hapi is calling reply() twice in one handler. Always make sure to add a return statement with your reply, as it should always be the last thing you do in your handler.

Cache

Here you can see cache headers for indicating to the browser how long this response may be cached for. This is different to the hapi application-level cache, which we will explore in later chapters.

Route configuration summary

The preceding descriptions of each part of a route configuration should give you the tools you need to cover for building some simple APIs in hapi. Let's look at a couple of things that happen in the background when we create a route, such as hapi's pattern matching and route ordering works. Understanding what happens underneath takes away a lot of the 'magic' when your application does something unexpected, or when you try to do something different to a typical, normal use case. After that, we'll look at how to return different types of content from your web server, such as HTML files or templates.

hapi routing algorithm

After learning about hapi's `server.route()` API and configuration object, you may have found yourself curious as to how is it possible to add all these routes, in a manner that allows to you to keep your codebase manageable. You may have the following questions in mind:

- Is it possible to have a route conflict?
- How are routes prioritized and mapped to a request?
- Is the order in which we register a route relevant?

Don't worry if you didn't have these questions, you'll have them soon enough. But let's answer them now.

hapi is one of the few frameworks in Node that have deterministic routing. Each request can only map to one route, and its routing table will be the same every time you start the server. This was one of the things that appealed to me initially, when I started working with Node and was researching Node frameworks in depth. As the application size and teams grow, routing conflicts become more of a concern, and I wanted to future-proof my work by starting with a framework that had a solid foundation. I found that the deterministic routing of hapi makes for a much more structured, enjoyable, and most importantly, safer approach to application development. If you have two routes that conflict, hapi will show an error on startup, providing details on the routes that conflict, making it much easier to debug and fix. This is much better than spending hours debugging this at runtime. If you have an editor open, I recommend trying to add a conflicting route and starting it so you can see what this error looks like.

This approach to routing is made possible by how hapi processes route definitions on startup. It takes all the route definitions, and creates a routing table where all routes are sorted from being most specific to most generic. You can read more about the path matching order in the API documentation at `http://hapijs.com/api#path-matching-order`.

When a request is received by the server, the hapi router (which is the call module, `https://github.com/hapijs/call`) iterates through this sorted routing table to find the first request it matches, and executes only that route.

This approach in routing is very different from that of express, Restify, and other frameworks through node. In those frameworks, routing is not deterministic. In Express, the routing table is organized by the order in which the routes are registered in the code. You can have two routes with the same or similar paths. If a request is received that matches multiple paths, it will execute each matching path.

To compare the two in code would look something like the following.

In hapi, where these `if else` loops are ordered based on most specific to generic, the code would be as follows:

```
if(request.match('/path/path1/{id}'/)) {
  return response;
} else if (request.match('/path/path2/{id}')) {
  return response;
} else if (request.match('/path')) {
  return response;
}
```

In Express, where the order is based on the order registered in the code, the code would be as follows:

```
if(request.match('/path/path/{id}'/)) {
  return response;
}
if (request.match('/path')) {
  return response;
}
if (request.match('/path/path2/{id}')) {
  return response;
}
```

These two design philosophies have an interesting trade-off.

With express, non-deterministic routing means that the route patterns can be more flexible, allowing for regular expressions. The downside of this is that the onus is on the developer to ensure that there are no routing conflicts, something which can be quite hard to test.

At this stage, you might notice a recurring theme: when faced with a choice, the design philosophies of hapi always aim to stay on the side of shifting responsibility from the developer to the framework by presenting errors at startup, and giving developers the tools to avoid making unnecessary mistakes.

The following points summarize this section on hapi's path processing:

- hapi uses deterministic routing
- problems with route configuration or conflicts will be demonstrated at startup, not at run time
- routes are sorted from being most specific to most generic, so where `server. route()` is called in, the code is not important

hapi request life cycle

After adding a few simple routes to your server, you will eventually come to the point where you need to add things like authentication, authorization, and have other use cases that need to be solved before your handler is ever reached. There are multiple approaches to this, such as creating a function to check authentication credentials, another for assigning authorization tokens that are called when every request is received initially by the handler. You could do this in the route prerequisites mentioned previously. However, if you forget to add these to a single route, or had something executed before your authentication function is called, you've left yourself open to secure data being accessible to unauthenticated users.

The approach which hapi uses to solve this is to have a well-defined request life cycle, with a reliable series of events that happen on every request. This gives you a fairly granular control over a request in an easy-to-extend and readable way.

The problem with the preceding approach of route or function ordering is that it is an implied life cycle, not a well-defined one, and is it is not always obvious where we are in the request life cycle. I see this with notes on modules such as `express-validator`, which must be called after `body-parser` or else the payload won't be validated, and no error will be thrown. This is a logic issue, not one related to code, and as such, there will be no errors for problems like this, which makes debugging a huge pain. I mentioned building infrastructure instead of application logic in the previous chapter, and this is a classic example of that.

With hapi, you don't have to worry about any of these things, because at all times you'll know where you are in the request life cycle. This is one feature that also makes it much easier to understand other codebases and the intention of the original developers when taking action on points within the request life cycle.

Let's look at the different stages in the request life cycle, bearing in mind that it is a lot to take in at once, and not necessary to remember. I often find myself returning to the API documentation to look up the event names to know when I want a certain action to take place, each time quite pleased that it was not my responsibility to implement, test, and document the life cycle I've built in each application. The full life cycle in the order of events can be found on hapijs.com at `http://hapijs.com/api#request-lifecycle`. I will cover it briefly here. So, when a request is received by a hapi server, it goes through the following events:

- The `onRequest` extension point is called.

  Every request will call this extension point. This is before any authentication, payload parsing, and so on is done. This extension point is unique in that it occurs before any route matching has occurred. The `request` object is decorated with the `request.setUrl()` and `request.setMethod()` methods, which can be used for rewriting requests only at this extension point.

- The next route matching occurs, based on `request.path`.

- Query extensions are processed (for example, JSONP), and cookies are parsed.

- The `onPreAuth` extension point is called.

  After the `onPreAuth` extension point, the request is authenticated. The payload is always parsed in this step so that payload authentication can also be performed.

- The `onPostAuth` extension point is called.

- Validation is then performed, first on the path parameters, the request query, and then the request payload.

- The `onPreHandler` extension point is called.

  After the `onPreHandler` extension point is called, the route prerequisites will be evaluated, and then the route handler itself.

- The `onPostHandler` extension point is called.

  Here `request.response` can be modified or a new response generated via a call to `reply()`. Usually, this would be to replace an error with an HTML page, like a 'not found' or internal server page.

- Next, the response payload is validated.

- The onPreResponse extension point is called.

  Again, as in the onPostHandler extension point, request.response can be modified or a new response generated via reply(). However, here the response will not go through the onPreResponse point to prevent an infinite loop.

- The response is then sent to the client, with the response event emitted.

- Finally, any tail actions are performed. tails are actions that the response sent to the client is not dependent on, and so may be performed after the response is sent. This could be something like updating a database, or adding audits to user actions in your application. You can read more about them in the API documentation at http://hapijs.com/api#requesttailname. When all tails are completed, a tail event is emitted.

Take note that some events are always called, and some are not. You may have not noticed the extension points throughout the life cycle; let's now look at how to add actions to extension points during different stages of the request life cycle.

Extending request life cycle events

Extending a request life cycle event has an easy-to-use API:

```
server.ext(event, method, [options])
```

So, if you wanted to log in to the console every time you received a request, it would be as follows:

```
...
server.ext('onRequest', function (request, reply) {
  console.log(`request received: ${request.}`);
  return reply.continue();
});
...
```

Note the function reply.continue() here—this is to return the control to the framework and indicate continuing with the request life cycle. The function reply() without continuing at this extension point would indicate that a response should be sent to the user from here, as it is likely there has been an error, and does not continue with the request life cycle. Not realizing this can be a common error when starting out with hapi. I will cover this in more detail when talking about the reply interface.

hapi request object

In hapi, the goal is never to monkey-patch or modify any of the normal Node objects or methods, but only to provide an extra layer around them to access the important parts.

Monkey patching is the method of overriding or extending the behavior of a method. For example, let's create an add function that returns the sum of two numbers:

```
let add = function (a, b) {
    return a + b;
}
```

We now want to log in to the console every time this is called, without altering the existing behavior. We would modify it by doing the following:

```
let oldAdd = add;
add = function (a, b) {
    console.log('add was called...');
    return oldAdd(a, b);
}
```

Now every time add is called, it will print add was called..., and return the sum just as before. This can be useful in modifying core language methods, but is not a recommended pattern, as it can cause very hard-to-debug side effects. I generally limit doing this to writing tests or debugging code.

This is the case with the hapi request object. The hapi request object I refer to here is the request parameter in the route handler's request, the reply signature. It contains all the information for an incoming request. As the request passes through the hapi life cycle, extra information will be added—we saw an example of this with route prerequisites earlier, and other information such as parsed cookies, authentication credentials, and the parsed payload—but the original request object is not modified and is accessible from request.raw.req. Along with the request data, some useful properties and functions are also available from the request object:

- request.server: This is the full server object accessible from within the route handler.

- request.generateResponse: This returns a response to be passed into the handler.

- `request.tail`: This adds a request tail task to be completed before the request life cycle, but after sending the response to the client. This is where you can do something like a database update, but shouldn't delay the response to the client, like adding audits after a request.

You can see the full `request` object description on hapijs.com at `http://hapijs.com/api#request-object`.

The reply interface

In the various life cycle events in hapi, such as authentication, route handlers, route prerequisites, you will see reply as one of the function arguments. This is the reply interface.

Throughout this book and the API documentation, you will see the function reply in two forms—either as `reply()` or as `reply.continue()`—which have two different purposes. `reply.continue()` is generally used to return the control flow back to the framework and continue through the request life cycle, whereas `reply()` is generally used to generate the response to be returned to the client. The only exception to this is inside the route prerequisites where `reply()` is used, as it assigns a variable to the `request.pre` object.

`reply()` can accept two parameters (error and response), but this is rarely used, as reply always acts on the first defined parameter that it is passed in. For example, if `reply()` is passed two variables and the first one is not null, it treats this as an error reply. If only one passed parameter is an error, it will do the same. If one non-error parameter is passed or there is a null or undefined parameter and a non-error parameter, it will consider it a normal response. To summarize:

```
// error with 500 status code
return reply(new Error());

// error with 500 status code
return reply(new Error(), 'success!');

// returns 'success!' with 200 status code
return reply(null, 'success!');

// returns 'success!' with 200 status code
return reply('success!');
```

If an error object is passed to `reply()`, it will wrap it in a `boom` error object.

boom is hapi's very handy error handling library. It provides a set of utilities for returning HTTP friendly errors. You can read more on boom on GitHub at `https://github.com/hapijs/boom`.

In fact, there are a various types to which `reply()` can be passed, which are very helpful when it comes to how you choose to handle your control flow (from hapijs.com):

- Null
- Undefined
- String
- Number
- Boolean
- Buffer object
- Error object
- Stream object (any Stream object must be compatible with the streams2 API and not be in objectMode)
- Promise object
- Any other object or array

Whatever type you pass to `reply()`, hapi will figure out what it needs to send in the response, such as payload, content-type, and status codes. There are examples of routes replying with all these types in the source code supplied with this book.

It is worth knowing that in a route handler when `reply()` is called, the response will not be sent to the client until the `process.nextTick()` callback.

 If you are unfamiliar with node's event loop and the `process.nextTick()` API, I suggest you watch this video by Philip Roberts, which provides a great explanation of the same: `https://www.youtube.com/watch?v=8aGhZQkoFbQ`.

Waiting on `process.nextTick()` enables you to make changes to the returned response before it is sent, improving code readability and simplifying route handler logic. This is useful when you want to specify the status code or content type instead of letting hapi figure it out.

This is common in catch all routes where you might want to return a special 'not found' page for requests that haven't matched another route. This would look something like the following:

```
...
server.route({
  method: '*',                                    // [1]
  path: '/{p*}          ',                         // [2]
  handler: function (request, reply) {
    return reply('The page was not found').code(404);   // [3]
  }
});
...
```

This is a good example to explore in detail, as it puts some of the concepts we discussed earlier in the chapter together. With reference to the line numbers given in the preceding code, let's go through the concepts:

- [1]: The HTTP method for this route. * is the wildcard, which means it can be any HTTP method.

- [2]: The path. here we used {p*}, where * is a wild card. This means that there can be zero or more path segments so that any combination of method and path will match this route. If you think back to the hapi routing algorithm, this is the most generic route definition possible, so will always be ordered last in the sorted routing table.

- [3]: The reply() function, where we alter the response before it is sent. Without the .code() at the end of the reply here, this route would return a plaintext response of 'The page was not found' with a status code of 200, which wouldn't really make sense. We could pass in a Boom.notFound() error object, or simply hard code the status code like we did here. The other things we can modify here are:

  ○ The content type:
    ```
    return reply('The page was not found').type('text/plain');
    ```

  ○ The headers:
    ```
    return reply(''The page was not found').header('X-Custom',
        'value');
    ```

Along with being able to modify responses before they are sent, we can modify the reply interface itself to provide custom functions for reducing boilerplate and make for more readable code. Let's look at the different ways this is commonly used in the next section.

Custom handlers

Now that we have some idea of what is happening under the hood before a request reaches our handler, and what happens after we call `reply()`, let's look at the different methods that hapi has for dealing with common use cases like static content. First it's good to know that it's actually possible to extend some of the interfaces in hapi like server and reply to get custom actions, for example:

```
...
const hello = function (name) {
  return this.response({ hello: name });
}
server.decorate('reply', 'hello', hello);
server.route({
  method: 'GET',
  path: '/{name}',
  handler: function (request, reply) {
    return reply.hello(request.params.name);
  }
});
...
```

The preceding code creates a new custom reply method called hello, which we can then call in our handlers. We can also do something similar with `server.handler()`, where we pass a different configuration object; this would look like the following:

```
...
// Defines new handler for routes on this server
server.handler('hello', (route, options) => {
  return function (request, reply) {
    const hello = options.customHello || 'Hello';
    const name = request.params.name;
    return reply(`${hello} ${name}`);
  }
});

server.route({
  method: 'GET',
  path: '/{name}',
  handler: {
    hello: {
      customHello: 'Welcome'
    }
  }
});
...
```

Fortunately, hapi provides plugins that, when registered, provide a range of custom reply methods and handlers for things like serving static content, proxies, and templating among many others. Let's look at the first of these for serving static file content: inert.

Serving static files with inert

inert (https://github.com/hapijs/inert) is the static file and directory handler module for hapi. It provides a lot of useful utilities for simplifying serving static content. Let's look at one of those now:

```
const Path = require('path');
const Hapi = require('hapi');
const Inert = require('inert');                        // [1]
const server = new Hapi.Server();
server.connection({ port: 3000 });
server.register(Inert, (err) => {                      // [2]
  server.route({
    method: 'GET',
    path: '/{param*}',
    handler: {                                         // [3]
      directory: {                                     // [3]
        path: Path.join(__dirname, 'public'),          // [3]
        listing: true                                  // [3]
      }                                                // [3]
    }                                                  // [3]
  });
  server.start((err) => {
    console.log(`Server running at: ${server.info.uri}`);
  });
});
```

Hopefully, this example is quite readable, and you begin to see the power of hapi's configuration-centric approach come into play here. Can you guess what this is before I explain the code? With reference to the numbers in the preceding code, let's go through it now line by line:

- [1]: First we require the inert module. You will need to run npm install if you are trying out this example.

- [2]: We register the inert plugin to the server.

- [3]: This is the new functionality `inert` has provided: a custom directory handler. Here we provide a directory configuration object which specifies the path to directory we plan to server static files from. In this example, the directory we serve content from is the `public` directory.

If you haven't figured it out yet, what we have built here is a static file server. Not bad for 25 lines of code! We also get to take advantage of the added security of hapi and inert here. A request to this route can only access files inside the public folder. Without this, an attacker could access files like the source code to this application, or worse, password files on the OS that this is running on—this is commonly referred to as a Directory Traversal Attack.

This is an example of the type of protection hapi offers out of the box when we say it is secure by default. Without knowing this type of security exploit, you are still guarded against it. This route will also return a 404 error if the file is not found, so you don't have to. Along with the directory handler, there is a custom file handler that works much like the aforesaid, but only serves a single file for a request instead of the files from a directory; it can be used as follows, something like a call-all not found route:

```
...
server.route({
  method: 'GET',
  path: '/{param*}',
  handler: {
    file: '404.html'
  }
});
...
```

`inert` also provides a decorated reply, `reply.file()`. This is useful when you need more granular control when serving files. Let's say, for example, if you only wanted to serve the HTML files from a directory from a certain handler, you could do something like the following:

```
...
server.route({
  method: 'GET',
  path: '/{file*}',
  handler: function (request, reply) {
    const path = `${request.params.file}.html`;
    return reply.file(path);
  }
});
...
```

Note that this doesn't give you directory traversal protection like the previous directory handler, so be aware that you will need to provide this yourself when using reply.file().

inert and hapi are very good at providing a lot of flexibility in working with static content. Let's look at combining inert and what we have learned about the hapi request life cycle to build a website that serves HTML pages, static images, and has a custom 404 page for bad links:

```
const Path = require('path');
const Hapi = require('hapi');
const Inert = require('inert');
const server = new Hapi.Server();
server.connection({ port: 80 });
server.register(Inert, (err) => {
  // serve static html and image files
  server.route({
    method: 'GET',
    path: '/{files*}',
    handler: {
      directory: {
        path: __dirname
      }
    }
  });

  // return not found page if handler returns a 404
  server.ext('onPostHandler', function (request, reply) {
    const response = request.response;
    if (response.isBoom && response.output.statusCode === 404) {
      return reply.file('./404.html').code(404);
    }
    return reply.continue();
  });

  server.start((err) => {
    console.log(`Server running at: ${server.info.uri}`);
  });
});
```

Hopefully, by now this is all starting to look familiar to you, as no new concepts have been introduced here. The addition here to the previous examples was the addition of an extension point on onPostHandler, which checks the response of the handler in the life cycle of the request. If the directory handler returned a 404, this extension point returns a 404 HTML page instead of a boom error object, else it continues with the request life cycle.

This covers most of what you need to know in terms of serving static content. If you would like to know more, I would encourage you to read more of the inert module documentation and source code, which is fortunately quite small.

Serving templates with vision

In most situations, when building a web application or website like that of the previous example, you won't just serve HTML files. Although some applications use this approach, where a single HTML is served, and then the JavaScript on the page interacts with the server through APIs to customize the page (commonly referred to as a Single Page App) which would be common in an AngularJS application, most web applications will customize the content served before is sent. This is commonly known as server-side rendering. There has been a lot of innovation in this area recently from client-side libraries such as React, where some of the page is rendered server-side and some on the client. These have been dubbed UniversalJS or Isomorphic JavaScript apps. Those concepts are worth knowing about, but are beyond the scope of this book.

What we will look at in this section is how to do server-side rendering, commonly called templating. In hapi, for templating support, much like with the static content support, we use a hapi plugin called `vision` (`https://github.com/hapijs/vision`), which provides all the utilities we need for templating or as vision refers to them: views.

When you register the `vision` plugin, it decorates the server, request, and reply interfaces with extra methods and utilities to simplify template rendering. Let's look at how to register and configure `vision` as well as add a route to serve some templates:

```
const Path = require('path');
const Hapi = require('hapi');
const Vision = require('vision');
const server = new Hapi.Server();
server.connection({ port: 1337 });
server.register(Vision, (err) => {          // [1]
  server.views({                            // [2]
    engines: {                              // [2]
      handlebars: {                         // [2]
        module: require('handlebars')       // [2]
      }                                     // [2]
    },                                      // [2]
    relativeTo: __dirname,                  // [2]
    path: 'templates'                       // [2]
  });                                       // [2]
```

```
server.route({
  method: 'GET',
  path: '/index',
  handler: function (request, reply) {
    let context = { title: 'Hapi Templates!' };
    return reply.view('index', context);          // [3]
  }
});
server.start((err) => {
  console.log(`Server running at: ${server.info.uri}`);
});
});
```

Some new concepts have been introduced in the preceding code, but overall it should largely look familiar at this stage. With reference to the numbers given in the code, let's go through some of the new concepts introduced therein:

- [1]: We register the Vision plugin, similar to the inert example. This provides us with the decorated server, request, and reply interfaces.

- [2]: We use the new server.views() interface to register a view engine. Although hapi supports most view engines, here we are using handlebars, as it is simple and widely used. Take note of the engines key here. Specifically, we are stating that handlebars is the templating engine for the HTML files here. Finally, we just specify where the templates are found.

- [3]: Here we use the new reply.view() interface. This is of the form reply.view(template, [context]) where the template is the file, and context is an object of values that will map to the placeholders in the template.

So for the previous example, let's create a template called index.html:

```
<html>
  <body>
    <h1>{{title}}</h1>
    <p>This is hard coded</p>
  </body>
</html>
```

With reply.view() called it would return the following:

```
<html>
  <body>
    <h1>Hapi Templates!</h1>
    <p>This is hard coded</p>
  </body>
</html>
```

Even though this is a very trivial example, it hopefully demonstrates clearly how simple templating is in hapi, and how powerful it can be in generating customized pages per request.

Let's look at some of the extra options for configuring template engines in hapi.

Vision configuration

For the full options available when configuring vision, I encourage you to read the module README.md at https://github.com/hapijs/vision, but I will briefly discuss the need-to-know parts here. These parts are as follows:

Engines

In order to use templates in hapi and vision, you have to register at least one templating engine, which will be the default for all file extensions. If more than one templating engine is registered, file extensions need to be matched to the templating engine, for example:

```
...
server.views({
  engines: {
    html: {
      module: require('handlebars')
    },
    jsx: {
      module: require('jsx')
    }
  }
  relativeTo: __dirname,
  path: 'templates'
});
...
```

Paths

The paths option in vision is for configuring the locations of all your template files. We have seen examples of some of these with relativeTo and path already.

Some templating engines like handlebars have methods for reducing boilerplate, and making it easier for breaking up templates such layouts, partials, and helpers. If you want to learn more about these, I recommend reading the description in the particular templating engine, but the good news is that they are also supported by vision.

compileMode

By default, `vision` assumes template engines to be synchronous, but asynchronous templating engines are also supported. If you are using a templating engine that requires an asynchronous render, just override the default when registering the engine as follows:

```
server.views({
  engines: {
    'html': {
      module: require('someasyncrenderingengine'),
      compileMode: 'async' // engine specific
    }
  }
});
```

Vision summary

This covers most of what you need to be able to render templates with hapi. Of course, templating is a much bigger topic, and I've only explored what you need to get started with templating here with hapi. To learn more about templating, I suggest you read more about the different templating methods today, like handlebars, dust, and jsx, which all attempt to simplify view rendering in their own ways.

 Like the last chapter, all code samples seen in here as well as some extra material can be found online in the repository available at `https://github.com/johnbrett/Getting-Started-with-hapi.js`. If you have any questions about the code samples in trying to understand code snippets or problems running them, feel free to open an issue.

Summary

In this chapter, we've introduced and looked in detail at routing in hapi. We looked at ways to add and configure routes in hapi. We've looked more in depth at the request life cycle and hapi's routing algorithm, the trade-offs they provide, how it affects our routing strategies, and where we can take advantage of them to simplify our application logic. We also looked at hapi's `request` object, and how it is modified throughout the request life cycle. Finally, we looked at the `reply` interface, how it can be extended, and how to use hapi plugins that extend the `reply` interface to cater to server static content and templating.

Hopefully, at this stage you have a good understanding of all the routing logic under the hood in hapi, feel comfortable adding and configuring multiple routes, and know how to add extension points to different points in hapi's request life cycle. You now have all the tools needed to create JSON APIs, static file servers, and websites using different templating language like handlebars.

In this chapter, we've also seen how to use some of the great plugins in the hapi ecosystem. In the next chapter, we will look at structuring your codebase when you have many routes and it starts getting unwieldy, using hapi's plugin API.

3
Structuring Your Codebase with Plugins

In the last two chapters, we introduced hapi, a server framework that simplifies developing servers in Node.js through a configuration-centric approach, and provides the tools needed to aid development where possible and stays out of the way when not needed.

We then looked at adding functionality to a hapi server, and looked at the tools needed to build APIs, web applications, and websites. During this, we touched on plugins, and the way in which we can use them to extend the functionality of servers.

In this chapter, we're going to look at methods and patterns for structuring an application as it grows, using plugins. This will involve taking a more in-depth look at the plugin API, so we can see what happens under the hood when we register a plugin, and how plugins can be used to break up the functionality of your server into smaller, more manageable parts.

By the end of this chapter, you will have the tools you need to grow an application codebase in hapi in a disciplined and structured manner, although it will take practice and experience for this to feel at ease when building an application. Let's get started.

Structuring applications

The way to structure an application is sometimes ignored when initially evaluating a framework in favor of how quickly we can get a 'hello world' example working, or the ability to quickly add features. In my opinion, this is a huge mistake as this borrows time later on in an application's life cycle; this is often known as technical debt. It leads to frustration, poor developer experience, and to a lot of required refactors that often degrade code quality. Furthermore, as teams scale, poor application infrastructure leads to much slower progress—adding features, longer time in getting new developers up-to-speed, and a higher tendency to create bugs with unknown side effects with every addition, change, or deletion of code. It is a well-documented fact that the number of bugs climbs linearly with the lines of code in a codebase, and it's understandably so—more the lines of code, more the opportunities a developer gets to make a mistake or create what I like to call implied knowledge. This is where a section of code appears to do something, but the real side effects of what it does, where it occurs in the code base, among other factors, are not obvious. They may be clear to the original developer, but to a new developer on a project, they are less so, and this generally leads to a lot of frustration.

Keeping the application logic structured and sensible without a strong knowledge of what you're doing is tougher in JavaScript and Node than most languages, and this can feel like a constant battle. Concepts such as control flow and error handling become painful if not managed early, and this is why I'm much more in favor of well-defined structures and consistent patterns when it comes to the layout of the code. hapi's request lifecycle and plugin API are good examples of this. Encapsulating your code inside a plugin gives it more context and structure, reducing the need for 'glue' code or implied knowledge.

I've found from the consistent structure which hapi's plugin API provides that hapi codebases are usually much easier to read, understand, and contribute to without any fear of breaking code or causing unknown side effects. I consider this a huge win for the framework—one of the most frustrating parts as a programmer is the phase of getting accustomed to a new code base. Reducing the time needed here makes for a much more productive and enjoyable experience as a developer. Let's look at the plugin API in more depth now.

hapi plugins

We've seen briefly in the previous chapters how to register third-party plugins to a hapi server, and the power that they have in being able to add custom handlers, routes, or print our routing table on startup. hapi's plugin system is powerful, extensive, and at the level where not only is the plugin system useful for integrating third-party modules, but also a great abstraction for breaking up your application into smaller, reusable chunks of code. Let's take one of our examples from the previous chapters, and show how we can break up our business logic into more manageable chunks using plugins.

Encapsulating functionality within plugins

If you remember, in the first chapter, we looked at what a full server with a single route added to it looks like, and used the `blipp` module to print the routing table on server start. In the example, all the code is contained in one entry file. As long as you have one route, this is fine; however, as an application grows, this practice leads to code with a structure that is harder to understand and follow.

In fact, as a rule when developing with hapi, I never put any business logic in my entry server file; all logic must be pushed into a plugin. This makes the code base much more readable, as all the code within the plugin now has context. Let's attempt this with an example, and create our first plugin. Let's start with a server very similar to the one we created in *Chapter 1, Introducing hapi.js*:

```
'use strict';
const Hapi = require('hapi');
const Blipp = require('blipp');
const server = new Hapi.Server();
server.connection({ port: 1337, host: '127.0.0.1' });
server.route({
  method: 'GET',
  path: '/hello',
  handler: function (request, reply) {
    return reply('Hello World\n');
  }
});
server.register(Blipp, (err) => {
  server.start((err) => {
    console.log(`Server running at ${server.info.uri}`);
  });
});
```

Here, the business logic that should be removed is that of adding a route to the server. This can be abstracted away to a plugin. Let's look at what is involved in creating our first plugin. First we will create a file that we will call `hello.js`, and in this, we'll add the code for our first plugin and our `/hello` route:

```
exports.register = function (server, options, next) {
  server.route({
    method: 'GET',
    path: '/hello',
    handler: function (request, reply) {
      return reply('Hello World\n');
    }
  });
  next();
};
exports.register.attributes = {
  name: 'hello'
};
```

Not too complicated, right? A hapi plugin is an object with a register function that accepts three parameters:

- `server`: It is a reference to the parent server object.
- `options`: It is an object of options that can be passed when registering the plugin (we'll look at this when registering our new plugin).
- `next`: It is a method to be called when you finish registering your plugin, and return the control back to the framework. While not used here, it's worth noting that it accepts one parameter, `err`, that should only be defined if there was an error registering the plugin. In practice, this is usually left undefined. This allows for plugins to do asynchronous operations when registering, which is hugely advantageous; we will explore this later.

The register function then has an attributes object attached to it for providing hapi with further information about the plugin.

Now that we have our own plugin, let's modify the original server example so that it now registers this new plugin instead of adding the `/hello` route. We'll also look in more detail at what happens when we call `server.register()`:

```
'use strict';
const Hapi = require('hapi');
const Blipp = require('blipp');
const Hello = require('./hello');
const server = new Hapi.Server();
```

```
server.connection({ port: 1337, host: '127.0.0.1' });
server.register([
  { register: Hello, options: {} },
  Blipp
], (err) => {
  server.start((err) => {
    console.log(`Server running at ${server.info.uri}`);
  });
});
```

Now we have successfully moved all our business logic to our plugin, and simplified our entry file. Hopefully, this makes for very readable code, and you're beginning to see how this could scale quite nicely as the codebase expands.

You might have noticed that we are passing an array to the register function now; this is because the register function can accept a single plugin object, or an array of plugin objects. The first plugin that we pass is our newly created plugin, `Hello`. The `options` object passed here maps to the second parameter in the plugin's `register` function. As we have no options that we need to pass in here, this has been left empty. When passed an array of plugins, the register function will iterate through each plugin, perform all actions in the `register` function until it reaches the `next()` call, and then move on to the next plugin. When all plugins are registered, it will finally call the callback passed to the `register` function, which, in this case, just starts our server.

Plugin options

There is a second optional object that you can pass to `server.register()` before the callback. These options are used by hapi, and are not to be confused with the `options` object we pass to a plugin.

The second `options` parameter allows you to configure some special options when registering a plugin, such as a route prefix, where the string provided will be prefixed to all the route paths registered within the plugin.

Another option that can be used is `vhost`, where the routes registered within the plugin will only be available to clients with a matching `vhost` in the request header.

Let's look at an example of plugin options in action. Let's add a prefix of `/v1` to the routes registered within our `Hello` plugin:

```
...
server.register(
  { register: Hello, options: {} },
```

```
  {
    routes: {
      prefix: '/v1'
    }
  }, (err) => {
  // start server
});
  ...
```

If we registered our plugins like this, our new `Hello` plugin would now register a route with the path `/v1/hello` instead of `/hello`. This can be very useful for versioning APIs.

Exposing and consuming plugins

In the previous section, we looked at how we can break up the business logic of our applications into smaller, more manageable chunks through plugins. We did this by attaching routes directly to the `server` object passed into the register, which is probably the simplest use case with plugins. But plugins won't always be used for just routing; you could perform logic on server start as with `blipp`, initialize database connections, create models for interacting with your data, and so on.

With developers still getting used to structuring server-side applications and the asynchronous nature of JavaScript, these types of use cases often are the beginning of messy or unstructured code due to the number of responsibilities placed on the developer. First of all, dependencies need to be acknowledged and dealt with in a sensible way — in the preceding examples, the database connection needs to be initialized before providing any model functionality. Secondly, we want a clean API where functionality is sandboxed in a consistent manner.

Fortunately, hapi provides APIs that support this with `server.dependency()` and `server.expose()`. Let's explore how to use these now.

Managing plugin dependencies

Let's make the previous example depend on another module requiring some form of persistent storage, for example, a database. Taking the plugin `hello.js`, let's modify it to add a dependency on a new plugin; we'll call `database` for this example:

```
exports.register = function (server, options, next) {
  server.dependency('database', (server, after) => {
    // Can do some dependency logic here.
    return after();
  });
```

```
    server.route({
      method: 'GET',
      path: '/hello',
      handler: function (request, reply) {
        return reply('Hello World\n');
      }
    });
    return next();
  };
  exports.register.attributes = {
    name: 'hello'
  };
```

In the preceding example, we see the new call to `server.dependency()`, which registers our dependency on the database plugin. Now when we try to start our server, it will fail with an error message making it clear that the `database` dependency wasn't respected. We would have to add this new `database` plugin before registering the `hello` plugin in our `server.register()`. This will also throw an exception if a circular dependency is detected, where a case of two plugins depending on each other may arise.

It is worth noting that multiple dependencies can be added here by passing an array of plugin names instead of one; this would look as follows:

```
...
server.dependency(['database', 'otherPlugin'], (after) => {
  return after();
});
...
```

There are multiple methods of registering plugin dependencies. If no dependency logic needs to be performed, there are two ways to synchronously register a plugin dependency. One is to use `server.dependency()` with no callback:

```
server.dependency(['database', 'otherPlugin']);
```

Or we can place the dependency in the `attributes` section of the plugin:

```
exports.register.attributes = {
  name: 'hello',
  dependencies: ['database', 'otherPlugin']
};
```

This is up to the preference of the developer; however, I usually opt for the first method, that is, via the `server.dependency` API. Often I find that I want to add logic after registering a dependency, so I prefer to keep all dependencies listed in one place in a consistent manner.

It is worth noting that for version management of plugins, npm peer dependencies (`http://blog.nodejs.org/2013/02/07/peer-dependencies/`) should be used, as hapi doesn't provide any native version management support.

Now that we have all the tools we need to nicely manage the dependencies of our plugins and business logic, let's look at the methods of combining them.

Exposing sandboxed functionality

Our plugin from the previous example is still quite trivial, as it only adds a route that returns a hard-coded string. Let's modify it so that it has some (very trivial!) functionality; we'll make it such that instead of just returning `hello world`, it returns a name if one is passed in:

```
exports.register = function (server, options, next) {
  const getHello = function (name) {
    const target = name || 'world';
    return `Hello ${target}`;
  };
  server.route({
    method: 'GET',
    path: '/hello/{name?}',
    handler: function (request, reply) {
      const message = getHello(request.params.name);
      return reply(message);
    }
  });
  next();
};

exports.register.attributes = {
  name: 'hello'
};
```

Now, as intended, we've added the ability to adjust the message to say hello to a name instead of world through the `getHello()` function. This is still pretty trivial, but what is not trivial is how you might use the function in another plugin or in the main server. One solution would be to make an npm module of the `getHello()` function that could be required in each plugin file, but this isn't always suitable. In this case, the function doesn't require any state and is quite simple, but in other cases it may use a database connection or depend on something else in the plugin. For these cases, you can use hapi's `server.expose()` function. With `server.expose()`, we can expose a plugin property so it is accessible through the following:

```
server.plugin['pluginName'].property;
```

Let's look at how we would expose the hello function now (with code removed for brevity):

```
...
const getHello = function(name) {
  const target = name || "world";
  return `Hello ${target}`;
};
server.expose({ getHello: getHello });
...
```

Now anywhere we have our server reference, we can use the `getHello()` function by calling:

```
server.plugins.hello.getHello('John'); // returns 'hello John'
```

This makes for a very clean and consistent API when sharing functionality from plugins. This is a very good example in which hapi provides the application infrastructure you need, so you can focus on building business logic, in a structured, clean, and testable manner.

Combining plugins

Let's make the preceding example a little less trivial to show that even with more complicated use cases, your code may remain readable and well structured. Instead of having just a route that responds with hello name, let's create a new plugin that lets us create and retrieve users from a persistent data store.

This means we'll need to add two routes, a POST and a GET route. They will have to interact with some persistent datastore, and finally expose the functionality so it can be used in other plugins. Sounds complicated? Let's see...

For this example, I will use LevelDB as the datastore. I use this as it's a simple in-process key-value data store that doesn't require any setup or configuration to start, and fortunately like with most databases or services, a plugin exists, making it very simple to use with hapi. If you're not familiar with LevelDB, I encourage you to check it out at `http://leveldb.org/`.

So let's begin with this example by creating our user management plugin that will add our routes and interact with LevelDB; we will put this in a file called `user-store.js`:

```
const Uuid = require('uuid');                         // [1]
const Boom = require('boom');                         // [2]
exports.register = function (server, options, next) {
  let store;                                          // [3]
```

```
server.dependency('hapi-level', (server, after) => {   // [3]
  store = server.plugins['hapi-level'].db;             // [3]
  return after();                                      // [3]
});                                                    // [3]
const getUser = function (userId, callback) {          // [4]
  return store.get(userId, callback);                  // [4]
};                                                     // [4]
const createUser = function (userDetails, callback) {  // [5]
  const userId = Uuid.v4();                            // [5]
  const user = {                                       // [5]
    id: userId,                                        // [5]
    details: userDetails                               // [5]
  };                                                   // [5]
  store.put(userId, user, (err) => {                   // [5]
    callback(err, user);                               // [5]
  });                                                  // [5]
};                                                     // [5]
server.route([
  {
    method: 'GET',                                     // [6]
    path: '/user/{userId}',                            // [6]
    config: {                                          // [6]
      handler: function (request, reply) {             // [6]
        const userId = request.params.userId;          // [6]
        getUser(userId, (err, user) => {               // [6]
          if(err) {                                    // [6]
            return reply(Boom.notFound(err));          // [6]
          }                                            // [6]
          return reply(user);                          // [6]
        });                                            // [6]
      },                                               // [6]
      description: 'Retrieve a user'                   // [6]
    },
    {
    method: 'POST',                                    // [7]
    path: '/user',                                     // [7]
    config: {                                          // [7]
      handler: function (request, reply) {             // [7]
        const userDetails = request.payload;           // [7]
        createUser(userDetails, (err, user) => {       // [7]
          if(err) {                                    // [7]
            return reply(Boom.badRequest(err));        // [7]
          }                                            // [7]
```

```
            return reply(user);                  // [7]
          });                                     // [7]
        },                                        // [7]
        description: 'Create a user'              // [7]
      }                                           // [7]
  ]);
  server.expose({                                 // [8]
    getUser: getUser,                             // [8]
    createUser: createUser                        // [8]
  });                                             // [8]
  return next();
};
exports.register.attributes = {
  name: 'userStore'
};
```

Despite the increase in example complexity, and the introduction of some new concepts, I still find this code quite readable and intuitive; hopefully, you do too. Let's go through it in more detail. With reference to the numbers in the code comments, let's go through each section:

- [1]: We are going to require the uuid npm module here so that we can create robust user IDs when creating users.

- [2]: We will also use the boom module from the hapi ecosystem so that we can provide HTTP-friendly error objects.

- [3]: Next we create a dependency on the hapi-level plugin. Inside the dependency callback, we assign our LevelDB reference to our store.

- [4]: getUser is a function we'll create for retrieving users from our LevelDB datastore. Of course, we could do this inside the handler, but abstracting it out makes for more readable code, and we can then expose this functionality later.

- [5]: Similar to getUser, we create a function for creating a user: createUser. In here, we use the uuid module to create a robust ID. Using the newly created ID and user details, we save our new user in LevelDB. We then pass any errors and the user object to our callback.

- [6]: We add our route for retrieving a user. As we've moved most functionality to the getUser function, the handler code is quite simple. We just take the userId from the request parameters, and use that as the key to look up our user.

- [7]: We add our route for creating a user. Again, this is very trivial as the heavy lifting is in the createUser function. We just pass in the request payload which contains all our user data to the createUser function, and reply with user created.

- [8]: Finally, our plugin will expose these methods. So anywhere that we have the server reference, we can reuse them with `server.plugins.userStore.getUser()` and `server.plugins.userStore.createUser()`, making for a nice clean API.

So, not too complicated right? Let's add this plugin to our server now, and we can get our application up and running:

```
'use strict';
const Hapi = require('hapi');
const Blipp = require('blipp');
const HapiLevel = require('hapi-level');                    [1]
const UserStore = require('./UserStore.js');               [2]
const server = new Hapi.Server();
server.connection({ port: 1337, host: '127.0.0.1' });
server.register([
  {                                                        [3]
    register: HapiLevel, options: {                        [3]
      config: { valueEncoding: 'json' }                    [3]
    }                                                      [3]
  },                                                       [3]
  UserStore,                                               [4]
  Blipp
], (err) => {
  server.start((err) => {
    console.log(`Server running at ${server.info.uri}`);
  });
});
```

Let's go through the changes to our `index.js` file in more detail here as well. With reference to the line numbers given with the preceding code, please find the explanation as follows:

- [1]: We require `hapi-level`, a useful micro library to create a LevelDB datastore, which exposes the LevelDB API through `server.plugins['hapi-level'].db`, and stores the reference in the variable `HapiLevel`.

- [2]: We require our new `UserStore` plugin.

- [3]: We register `HapiLevel`, and pass it some configuration. We specify a value encoding of JSON, which means our datastore will now store and return JSON instead of the default UTF8 encoding.

- [4]: Finally, we register our new `UserStore` plugin.

So, without too many changes to our server, we now have a fully functioning user store API that accepts and returns JSON, with a very easy to understand and manage codebase. When you start the server, it will log our routes with description thanks to `blipp`, so you should see the following:

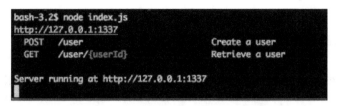

```
bash-3.2$ node index.js
http://127.0.0.1:1337
    POST    /user                    Create a user
    GET     /user/{userId}           Retrieve a user

Server running at http://127.0.0.1:1337
```

A great exercise here to increase your learning of hapi and of application structure in general, would be to try and add functionality to this server for updating and deleting users. I encourage you to try this now.

In this example, we've demonstrated some of the advantages that plugins provide us. In our applications, they are useful for breaking up application logic into reusable application building blocks. They also make for an easy-to-use way of integrating third-party libraries within your application, as we saw with `hapi-level`. When and where to use plugins is always an interesting debate, and there's no clear guideline given. It's up to the application developers like you. There is no clear best strategy, as every application is different.

The hapi plugin ecosystem

We've already seen how easy and useful it can be to integrate third-party libraries in hapi with the usage of `blipp` and `hapi-level` in the previous examples. Let's look at the other plugins that are available in the hapi ecosystem. The list I've gathered here is certainly not exhaustive; these are only a few pulled out from the hapijs.com website just to showcase the wide range of plugins available in the ecosystem; for the full list, visit `hapijs.com/plugins` or visit `https://hapi-plugins.com/`, a searchable database of hapi plugins.

Authentication

Authentication will be covered in detail in *Chapter 5, Securing Applications with Authentication and Authorization*, so we won't go into detail on these plugins here, but it's good to be aware that there are plugins in the hapi ecosystem that do the heavy lifting in terms of authentication, such as parsing request headers or cookies. A few of these plugins are as follows:

- `hapi-auth-basic`: An authentication scheme for authenticating requests supplied with a username and password combination.

- `hapi-auth-cookie`: An authentication scheme that provides simple cookie-based session management.

- `bell`: A third-party logic plugin that ships with support for authentication with a third-party service such as GitHub, Twitter, or Facebook.

Documentation generation

Documentation is always a painful part of development. It doubles the work of the developer, as they must write code and the matching documentation. Keeping the two in sync is often painful. I find that if at any stage in the development cycle, you have to repeat yourself, you're usually doing something unnecessary, and the following plugin proves that. When registered, it generates documentation based on route configuration:

- `hapi-swagger`: A documentation generation plugin. It self-documents all APIs based on the supplied route configuration with interactive swagger documentation.

Logging

For production systems, logging is of the utmost importance, and unfortunately, is often neglected until too late. The following plugins make logging for hapi servers much easier:

- `blipp`: We have seen this one already; it displays the routing table on server start.

- `good`: A logging plugin that supports multiple outputs. We will cover this plugin in more detail in *Chapter 7, Making Your Application Production Ready*.

Utilities

These are extra plugins from the hapi universe that demonstrate the flexibility and power of hapi's plugin system:

- `inert`: The file handler plugin we looked at in *Chapter 2, Adding Functionality by Routing Requests*

- `vision`: The template rendering support plugin that we looked at in *Chapter 2, Adding Functionality by Routing Requests*

- `nes`: A websocket adapter plugin for hapi for building real-time applications with hapi

- `h2o2`: A proxy handler plugin
- `bassmaster`: This adds a batch endpoint that makes it easy to combine multiple requests into a single one
- `tv`: An interactive debug console plugin for hapi servers

These are just a few plugins; there are many more, and I encourage you to take a look now and experiment with them.

Composing applications from plugins

So far in this chapter, we've looked at how to create plugins, how to use third-party plugins in our applications, how to add communication between plugins, and how to create dependencies between plugins.

Plugins are a great way of managing your code base by splitting it up into smaller, more manageable chunks of functionality. But like every design strategy, plugins have some downsides. The downsides are mainly in the form of extra overhead when it comes to our registering and configuring them for our applications. In fact, configuration alone can be a big headache for applications. Let's look at how we can mitigate this.

When you think back to our `index.js` entry file from the last example, we simplified this by pushing all our business logic to plugins, making for a very readable and easy-to-follow entry file for new users of our codebase.

But now let's think about how this scales. As more functionality is added, the number of plugins would obviously grow. As an application moves closer to production, we would also want to add features such as logging and caching, which would mean even more plugins and further configuration. For larger applications, we could quickly form a giant entry or `index.js` file comprised of large configuration objects for our servers, connections, and repeated nested calls to `plugin.register()`.

Fortunately for us, in keeping with the theme of configuration-over-code and foresight from the hapi team, the `server.compose()` API was created in the very first version of hapi. This allows you to create and configure your entire server, connections (or packs as they were called then), and plugins, all from just a single configuration object.

As hapi grew and became more modular, `server.compose()` was removed, and the compose functionality was pushed to a module called `glue` (`https://github.com/hapijs/glue`).

Using `glue`, we can define our entire application from this single configuration object. This can be a hard concept to grasp without an example, so let's take our previous user store example, and reduce it to a single configuration object that can be passed to `glue` to compose our server for demonstrating how this works. If you want to run this example, don't forget to `npm install glue` first! Let's see what our entry file looks like now:

```
const Glue = require('glue');
const manifest = {
  server: {},
  connections: [
    { port: 1337, host: '127.0.0.1' }
  ],
  plugins: [
    { 'hapi-level': { path: './temp', config: { valueEncoding:
      'json' } } },
    { './user-store.js': {} },
    { 'blipp': {} }
  ]
}
Glue.compose(manifest, { relativeTo: __dirname }, (err, server) => {
  server.start((err) => {
    console.log(`Server running at ${server.info.uri}`);
  });
});
```

Hopefully, it's clear from this example that all our server creation and configuration code has been moved to this new `manifest` object, which we then pass to `glue.compose()`. This then composes our server object from the configuration, and returns the server object as the second parameter of the compose callback function. On reading `manifest`, you might be able to spot the one-to-one mapping of configuration against the actual hapi methods, but let's go through the mappings here:

```
{
  server: {},
  // maps to `new Hapi.Server();`

  connections: [{ port: 1337, host: '127.0.0.1' }],
  // maps to server.connection({ port: 1337, host: '127.0.0.1' });

  plugins: [ ... ]
  // maps to server.register([ ... ]);
}
```

While the reduction in code isn't huge in this example as our server is still quite small, you can imagine this saving quite a considerable amount of code when you have multiple connections and plugins registered to each.

Moreover, a command-line tool that uses `glue` internally can be used to launch a hapi server just from the `manifest` configuration object called `rejoice` (`https://github.com/hapijs/rejoice`). With this, instead of using `glue` within our application, we can just export the `manifest` object from our `index.js` file, and then use `rejoice` from the command line to compose and launch our server.

Again, this is best demonstrated by an example. So, let's modify the preceding example so that instead of passing our `manifest` object to `glue.compose()`, we export it using `module.exports` to be able to launch the server directly from the command line using `rejoice`:

```
const manifest = {
  server: {},
  connections: [
    { port: 1337, host: '127.0.0.1' }
  ],
  plugins: [
    { 'hapi-level': { path: './temp', config: { valueEncoding:
      'json' } } },
    { './user-store.js': {} },
    { 'blipp': {} }
  ]
};
module.exports = manifest;
```

Hopefully, this is still easy to follow. The only change in this example from the previous one is that this time we used `module.exports` to export the `manifest` object instead of passing it to `glue.compose()`.

Next, we need to be able to run rejoice from the command line. So, let's first install it using the following command:

$ npm install rejoice

This installs rejoice along with the **commandline interface** (CLI) tool within our `node_modules` folder. Usually, CLI tools in `npm` packages are located within the `/bin` directory of a module, and `rejoice` is no different. To launch our application, now we use the following command:

$ ./node_modules/rejoice/bin/rejoice -c index.js -p ./

This command does a number of things, so let's explain them. First, it calls `rejoice`; it also specifies `index.js` as the configuration object source using the `-c` flag, and then that our plugin files (in this case, the `user-store.js` file) are in the current directory, using the `-p` flag. All going well, if you run this command, you will get the following:

```
bash-3.2$ ./node_modules/rejoice/bin/rejoice -c index.js -p .
http://127.0.0.1:1337
    POST    /user                              Create a user
    GET     /user/{userId}                     Retrieve a user
```

A couple of notes on this: instead of creating your server object in a `.js` file and exporting it using `module.exports`, you could also pass in a JSON file directly. This is up to developer preference, as is using `glue` and `rejoice` at all. Plenty of projects I've seen don't use either, but as projects grow, `glue` and `rejoice` are a great way of keeping your entry file simple, so it's good to be aware of them.

Now, you also might have found typing `./node_modules/rejoice/bin/rejoice` constantly to launch your application frustrating. Fortunately, with npm scripts we have some alternatives to this, and we will explore these in detail in the next chapter on testing when we look at setting up our test scripts.

Summary

Like the last chapter, all code samples seen here as well as some extra material can be found online in the repository available at `https://github.com/johnbrett/Getting-Started-with-hapi.js`. This chapter had more code than the previous chapters, so I encourage you to take a deeper look, run some examples, and try expanding them where possible. If you have any questions about the code samples in trying to understand the code snippets, or have problems running them, feel free to open an issue.

In this chapter, we looked at the different ways we can structure a code base with hapi using some of the tools provided by the hapi ecosystem, such as plugins. We looked in detail at the plugin API, how to write our own plugins, how to integrate third-party plugins, manage dependencies, and facilitate communication between plugins with `server.expose()`. We also took a quick look at the some of the plugins in the hapi ecosystem.

Finally, we looked at alternative methods of managing our server, connection, and plugin configuration by reducing it to a single configuration object. We then covered multiple ways of launching our applications using this configuration object by using two modules from the hapi ecosystem: `glue` and `rejoice`.

Hopefully, at this stage you have a basic understanding of how you would add more functionality to a hapi server while keeping the code structured and manageable.

In the next chapter, we'll take a step closer to making a server production ready by looking at testing, and the importance of test coverage.

4
Adding Tests and the Importance of 100% Code Coverage

In this chapter, we are going to explore the topic of testing in Node and hapi. We will look at writing a simple test using hapi's test runner lab, testing hapi applications, techniques to make testing easier, and finally, achieving the all-important 100% code coverage.

Testing is often a contentious issue when it comes to development. There are different attitudes towards its importance and relevance in the development cycle. Some developers believe in a Test-driven Development model, where tests should be written first. Others write tests while developing or wait till development is complete, then try and reach 100% code coverage with their tests. Unfortunately, in most cases, many don't bother with any at all, usually with what I believe to be as the naive view that "there isn't enough time to write tests".

 Code coverage is the percentage of lines of application code that are executed by a testing suite.

Most of my career has actually been spent with the latter point of view, but working with hapi and seeing the benefits by focusing on testing throughout the ecosystem has shown me the light in this regard. In the hapi ecosystem, testing and 100% code coverage are paramount, and no code change to any module within the ecosystem will be accepted if the change isn't accompanied by the tests required to keep code coverage at 100% — a rule I now apply to all my own modules on npm.

You might ask why is testing and 100% coverage so important? What are its advantages? And if testing is so important, why is it often overlooked? Let's explore those questions now, starting with the latter.

Why is the importance of testing overlooked?

In my experience, most development comes from two motivations: employment or recreation. There are others such as creating open source software (like hapi), research, and the like, but most of them fall under the aforementioned two categories. The motivation behind both categories is usually result-focused; when the motivation is employment, we aim to generate a monetary value from the code that we write. In case it is recreational, we are often exploring a new technology and just want to build something for a demo or to learn the inner workings of a new framework or library. It's easy to see how writing tests doesn't fit into either category.

In case of development for employment, tests aren't a sellable feature of software and are expensive. They take a lot of time and money to design, write, maintain, run, and keep up-to-date with best practices. Often, the size of a testing codebase will be larger than that of the codebase it is testing. The thought process here is usually: what's the return on investment? When we've deadlines to meet, why would time be spent on writing and maintaining code that can't monetized. So usually, the thought process is "manual testing is enough".

With recreational development, our focus is often on doing something quickly, learning that new language or framework, or quickly prototyping that app we want to demonstrate. We don't have the time to write tests. Tests aren't fun either, why write them?

Unfortunately, the downside to not writing tests is that we become better at developing code and worse at testing. I believe a lack of emphasis on testing makes us inefficient and less productive developers. Why? I'll explain this is the next section.

The benefits and importance of testing code

I mentioned the concept of technical debt in the previous chapter, which, as a reminder, is the building up of work that must be done before a particular job is complete, making changes much harder to implement in the future. A codebase without tests is a clear indication of a technical debt. Let's explore this statement in more detail.

Even very simple applications will generally comprise of the following:

- Features, which the end user interacts with
- Shared services such as authentication and authorization that features interact with

These will all generally depend on some direct persistent storage, or API. And finally, for implementing most of these features and services, we will use libraries, frameworks, and modules, regardless of language. So even for simpler applications, we have arrived at a few dependencies to manage already, where a breaking change in one could possibly break everything up in the chain.

So let's take a common use case in which a new version of one of your dependencies is released. That could be a new hapi version, a smaller library, your persistent storage engine, MySQL, MongoDB, or even an operating system or language version. SemVer, as mentioned in the first chapter, attempts to mitigate this somewhat, but you are taking someone at their word that they have adhered to this correctly, and SemVer is not used everywhere. So, in the case of a breaking change, the following questions arise:

- Will the current application work with this new dependency version? What fails?
- What percentage of tests fail?
- What's the risk if we don't upgrade?
- Will support eventually be dropped, including security patches?

Without a good automated test suite, these have to be answered by manual testing, which is a huge waste of developer time. Development progress stops here each time these tasks have to be done, which means that these type of tasks are rarely done, building further technical debt. Apart from that, humans have been proven to be poor at repetitive tasks, prone to error, and I know I personally don't enjoy manual testing, which makes me poor at it. I view repetitive manual testing as time wasted, as these questions could easily be answered by running a test suite against the new dependency so that developer time could be spent on something more productive.

Now let's look at a worse and still common example; a security exploit has been identified in one of your dependencies. As mentioned previously, if it's not easy to update, you won't do it often so you could be on an outdated version that won't receive this security update. Now you have to jump multiple versions at once, scrambling to test them manually. This usually means many quick fixes, which often just cause more bugs. In my experience, code changes under pressure are what deteriorate the structure and readability in a codebase, leading to a greater number of bugs, and are a clear sign of poor planning.

A good development team, instead of looking at what is currently available, will look ahead to what is in beta, and will know ahead of time if they expect to run into issues. The questions asked will be: will our application break in the next version of Chrome? The next version of Node? hapi does this by running the full test suite against future versions of Node, alerting the Node community of how planned changes would impact hapi and the Node community as a whole. This is what we should all aim to do as developers.

A good test suite has even bigger advantages when working in a team, or when adding new developers to a team. Most development teams start out small and then grow, which means that all the knowledge of the initial development needs to be passed onto new developers joining the team. So, how do tests benefit here?

- Tests are great documentation on how the various parts of the application work for other members of a team. When trying to communicate a problem in an application, a failing test is a perfect illustration of what and where the problem is.

- When working as a team, for every code change made by you or another member of the team, you're faced with the aforementioned problem of changing a dependency. Do we just test the changed code? What about the code that depends on the code changed? Is it going to be manual testing again? If this is the case, how much time in a week would be spent on manual testing versus development. Often, with changes, the existing functionality can be broken with the new functionality, which is called **regression**. Having a good test suite highlights this and makes it much easier to prevent. These are the questions and topics that need to be answered when discussing the importance of tests.

- Writing tests can also improve code quality. For one, identifying dead code is much easier when having a good testing suite. If you find you can only get 90% code coverage, what does the extra 10% do? Is it used at all if it's unreachable? Does it break other parts of the application if removed? Writing tests will often improve your skills in writing more maintainable code.

- Software applications usually grow to be complex pretty quick; it happens, but we always need to be active in dealing with this or software complexity will win. A good test suite is one of the best tools we have to tackle this issue.

This is not an exhaustive list on the importance of benefits of writing tests for your code, but hopefully, it has convinced you of the importance of having a good testing suite. So now that we know why we need to write good tests, let's look at hapi's test runner lab and assertion library code, and how, along with some tools from hapi, they make writing tests a much easier and a more enjoyable experience.

Introducing hapi's testing utilities

The test runner in the hapi ecosystem is called `lab`. If you're not familiar with test runners, they are a **Command-line Interface** (**CLI**) tool for running your testing suite. It is inspired by a similar test tool called `mocha`, and in fact, initially began as a fork of the `mocha` codebase. But as hapi's needs diverged from the original focus of `mocha`, `lab` was born.

`code` is the assertion library commonly used in the hapi ecosystem. An assertion library forms the part of a test that performs the actual checks to judge whether a test case has passed or not, for example, checking if the value of a variable is true after an action has been taken.

Let's look at our first test script, then we can take a deeper look at `lab` and `code`, how they function under the hood, and some differences they have with other commonly-used libraries such as `mocha` and `chai`.

Installing lab and code

You can install `lab` and `code` the same way as any other module on npm:

```
npm install lab code --save-dev
```

Note the `--save-dev` flag added to the preceding `install` command. Remember your `package.json` file, which describes an npm module? This adds the modules to the `devDependencies` section of your `package.json` file. `devDependencies` are dependencies that are required for the development and testing of a module, but are not required for using the module.

The reason why these are separated is that when we run `npm install` in an application codebase, it only installs the dependencies and `devDependencies` of the `package.json` in that directory. For all the modules installed, only their dependencies are installed, not their development dependencies. This is because we only want the dependencies required to run that downloaded application; we don't need all the development dependencies for every module downloaded as well.

The command `npm install` installs all the dependencies and `devDependencies` of `package.json` in the current working directory, and only the dependencies of those get installed, not `devDependencies`. To get the development dependencies of a particular module, navigate to the root directory of the module and run `npm install`.

After you have installed `lab`, you can then run it with:

```
./node_modules/lab/bin/lab test.js
```

This is quite long to type every time, but fortunately, due to a handy feature of npm called npm scripts, we can shorten it. If you look at `package.json` generated by the `npm init` in the first chapter, depending on your version of npm, you may see the following within (some code removed for brevity):

```
...
"scripts": {
  "test": "echo \"Error: no test specified\" && exit 1"
},
...
```

The npm scripts are a list of commands related to the project; they can be for testing like we will see in this example, for starting an application, for build steps, and for starting extra servers, among many other options. They offer huge flexibility in how these are combined for managing the scripts related to a module or application. I could spend a chapter or even a book on just these, but they are outside the scope of this book, so let's just focus on what is important to us here. If you would like to learn more, the hoodie team have an excellent comprehensive introduction to npm scripts at `https://github.com/hoodiehq/hoodie-css/blob/feature/build-automation/DEVELOPMENT.md`.

To get a list of available scripts for a module application, run the following command in the project directory:

```
$ npm run
```

To then run any of the listed scripts, such as `test`, you can just use the following command:

```
$ npm run test
```

As you can see, this gives a very clean API for scripts and the context for each of them in the project's `package.json`. From this point on in this book, most code snippets will use npm scripts for testing or running any examples. We should strive to use these in our projects to simplify and document the commands related to applications and modules for ourselves and others.

Let's now add the ability to run a test file to our `package.json`. This just requires modifying the scripts section as follows:

```
...
"scripts": {
  "test": "./node_modules/lab/bin/lab ./test/index.js"
},
...
```

 It is a common practice in Node to place all tests within the test directory of a project.

A handy addition to note here is that when calling a command with `npm run`, the `bin` directory of every module in your `node_modules` directory is added to PATH when running these scripts; so, we can actually shorten this script to:

```
...
"scripts": {
  "test": "lab ./test/index.js"
},
...
```

If you remember the last chapter where we used `rejoice` to launch our applications, we could also have created an npm script to start our application. As in the preceding example, taking advantage of the `bin` directory of every module in the `node_modules` directory being added to PATH, this could also have been shortened as follows:

```
...
"scripts": {
  "start": "rejoice -c index.js -p ."
},
...
```

Hopefully, this demonstrates the advantage of using npm scripts. Once inside the application directory, a simple call to `npm run`, and they are given the commands to start the application, or run it's testing suite, like a free form of documentation. You can imagine how, when looking at a new project or module, developers especially, might not know what test runner is used by this project, or what rejoice is, or how to normally start a project. When the npm scripts are in place, as shown in this section, people new to the project don't have to be aware of what the underlying tools are unless they want to.

Local versus global modules

When npm modules are installed like we saw in the previous section, run the following command:

```
$ npm install lab
```

It is considered local, as the module is installed within the project directory from which the command is being run. While I believe this is how we should all install our modules, it is worth pointing out that it is possible to also install a module globally. This means that when installing something such as lab, it is immediately added to PATH and can be run from anywhere. We do this by adding a -g flag to the install:

```
$ npm install lab -g
```

This may appear handier than having to add npm scripts or run commands locally, outside of an npm script, but it should be avoided where possible. Often installing globally requires sudo to run, which means you are taking a script from the internet, and allowing it to have complete access to your system. Hopefully, the security concerns here are obvious.

Other than that, different projects may use different versions of test runners, assertion libraries, or build tools, which can have unknown side effects, and cause debugging headaches.

The only time I would use globally installed modules are for command-line tools that I may use outside a particular project, such as a Node-based terminal text editor such as slap (https://www.npmjs.com/package/slap) or a process manager such as PM2 (https://www.npmjs.com/package/pm2)—but never with sudo!

Now that we are familiar with installing lab and code and the different ways of running it inside and outside of npm scripts, let's look at writing our first test script, and take a more in-depth look at lab and code.

Our first test script

Let's take a look at what a simple test script in lab looks like, using the code assertion library. Let's create a fresh directory for the examples in this chapter. Create a directory called example-1, and within that another directory called test. As mentioned earlier, in Node, generally all tests are located within the /test directory of a project. Let's create a file called index.js within our new /test directory, and add the following:

```
const Code = require('code');                    [1]
const Lab = require('lab');                       [1]
```

```
const lab = exports.lab = Lab.script();          [2]
lab.experiment('Testing example', () => {        [3]
  lab.test('fails here', (done) => {             [4]
    Code.expect(false).to.be.true();             [4]
      return done();                             [4]
  });                                            [4]
  lab.test('passes here', (done) => {            [4]
    Code.expect(true).to.be.true();              [4]
    return done();                               [4]
  });                                            [4]
});
```

This preceding script, even though small, includes a number of new concepts; so let's go through it with reference to the numbers given with the code:

- [1]: Here we just include the `code` and `lab` modules as we would any other Node module.

- [2]: As mentioned before, it is a common convention to place all test files within the `test` directory of a project. However, there may be JavaScript files in the `test` directory that aren't tests, and therefore, should not be tested. To avoid this, we inform `lab` of which files are the test scripts by calling `Lab.script()` and assigning the value to `lab` and `exports.lab`.

- [3]: The `lab.experiment()` (aliased `lab.describe()`) is just a way to group tests neatly. In test output, tests will have the experiment string prefixed to the message, for example, "Testing example fails here". However, this is optional.

- [4]: These are the actual test cases. Here we define the name of the test and pass a callback function with the parameter function done. We see the assertion library code in action here for managing our assertions. And finally, we call the `done` function when finished with our test case.

The main things to note here are that `lab` tests are always asynchronous. In every test, we have to call `done()` to finish the test; there is no counting of function parameters or checking if the synchronous functions have completed to ensure that a test is finished. Although this requires the boilerplate of calling the `done` function at the end of every test, it means all tests, synchronous or asynchronous, have a consistent structure.

In chai, which was originally used for hapi, some of the assertions such as `.ok`, `.true`, and `.false` used properties instead of functions for assertions, while assertions such as `.equal()` and `.above()` used functions. This type of inconsistency leads to easily forgetting that an assertion should be a method call, and omitting the `()`. This means the assertion is never called, and the test may pass as a false positive. code's API is more consistent in that every assertion is a function call; here is a comparison of the two:

- Chai:

```
expect('hello').to.equal('hello');
expect(foo).to.exist;
```

- Code:

```
expect('hello').to.equal('hello');
expect('foo').to.exist();
```

Notice the difference in the second `exist()` assertion. In chai, you see the property form of the assertion, while in code you see the required function call here. Through this, lab can make sure that all assertions within a test case are called before `done` is complete, or it will fail the test.

So lets try running our first test script. As we already updated our package.json script, we can run our test with:

```
$ npm run test
```

And this will generate the following output:

```
> lab test/index.js



  x.

Failed tests:

  1) Testing examples fails here:

     Expected false to be true

     at /Users/johnbrett/github/Getting-Start-with-Hapi.js/Chapter 4 - Testing/example-1/test/index.js:10:38


1 of 2 tests failed
Test duration: 21 ms
No global variable leaks detected
```

There are a couple of things to note from this. Tests run are symbolized with a . or an x, depending on whether it passed or not. You can have lab list the full test title by adding the -v or --verbose flag to our npm test script command.

 There are lots of flags to customize the run and output of lab, so I recommend using the full labels for each of these, for example, --verbose, and --lint instead of -v or -l to save you from referring back to the documentation each time.

You may have noticed the **No global variable leaks detected** message at the bottom. lab assumes the global object shouldn't be polluted, and checks that no extra properties have been added after running tests. lab can be configured to not run this check, or whitelist certain globals. Details of this are in the lab documentation at https://github.com/hapijs/lab.

Testing approaches

I mentioned earlier the concept of **TDD** or **Test-driven Development**. This is one of the many approaches known for building a test suite, as is **BDD** (**Behavior-driven Development**), and like most test runners in Node, lab is unopinionated in how you structure your tests. Details of how to structure your tests in a TDD or BDD can again be found easily in the lab documentation.

Testing hapi applications with lab

As I mentioned earlier, testing is considered paramount in the hapi ecosystem, with every module in the ecosystem having to maintain 100% code coverage at all times, as with all module dependencies.

Fortunately, hapi provides us with some tools to make the testing of hapi apps much easier through a module called shot, which simulates network requests to a hapi server. Taking our first example of the hello world server given in *Chapter 1, Introducing hapi.js*, let's write a simple test for it:

```
const Code = require('code');
const Lab = require('lab');
const Hapi = require('hapi');
const lab = exports.lab = Lab.script();
lab.test('It will return Hello World', (done) => {
  const server = new Hapi.Server();
  server.connection();
  server.route({
    method: 'GET',
```

```
      path: '/',
      handler: function (request, reply) {
        return reply('Hello World\n');
      }
  });
  server.inject('/', (res) => {
    Code.expect(res.statusCode).to.equal(200);
    Code.expect(res.result).to.equal('Hello World\n');
    done();
  });
});
```

Now that we are more familiar with what a test script looks like, most of this will look familiar. However, you may have noticed we never made a call to `server.start()` in the test. This means the server was never started and no port assigned, but we can still make requests against it using the `server.inject()` API. Not having to start a server means less setting up and tearing down before and after tests, and that a test suite can run quicker, as less resources are required. `server.inject()` will still be used if with the same API irrespective of whether the server has been started or not. The `server.inject()` API is provided via the `shot` module (`https://github.com/hapijs/shot`), if you would like to read more about how the API works under the hood.

Code coverage

As I mentioned earlier in the chapter, having 100% code coverage is paramount in the hapi ecosystem, and in my opinion, hugely important for any application to have. Without a code coverage target, writing tests can feel like an empty or unrewarding task, where we don't know how many tests are enough, or how much of our application or module has been covered. With any task, we should know what our goal is; testing is no different, and that is what code coverage gives us. Even with 100% coverage, things can still go wrong, but it means at the very least, every line of code has been considered and has at least one test covering it. I've found from working on modules for hapi that trying to achieve 100% code coverage actually gamifies the process of writing tests, making it a more enjoyable experience overall.

Fortunately, lab has code coverage integrated, so we don't need to rely on an extra module to achieve this. It's as simple as adding the `--coverage` or `-c` flag to our test script command. Under the hood, lab will then build an abstract syntax tree so it can evaluate the lines to be executed for producing our coverage, which will be added to the console output when we run tests. The code coverage tool will also highlight the lines that are not covered by tests, so you know what has not been tested. This is extremely useful in identifying where to focus your testing effort.

It is also possible to enforce a minimum threshold as to the percentage of code coverage required to pass a suite of tests with `lab` through the `--threshold` or `-t` flag, followed by an integer. This is used for all the modules in the hapi ecosystem, and the threshold is set to 100, implying 100%.

Having a threshold of 100% for code coverage makes it much easier to manage the changes in a codebase. When any update or pull request is submitted, we can run the test suite against the changes, and know that all tests pass and all the code is covered before we even look at what has been changed in the proposed submission. There are services that even automate this process for us such as Travis CI (`https://travis-ci.org/`).

It's also worth knowing that the coverage report can be displayed in a number of formats; I suggest reading the lab documentation for a full list of these reports with explanations which is available at `https://github.com/hapijs/lab`.

Let's now look at what's involved in getting 100% coverage for our previous example. First of all, we'll move our server code to a separate file, which we will place in the `/lib` directory, and call `index.js`.

It's worth noting here that not only is it a good testing practice but also a typical module structure in the hapi ecosystem to place all module code in a directory called `lib`, and the associated tests for each file within `lib`, in the `test` directory, preferably with a one-to-one mapping like we have done here, where all the tests for `lib/index.js` are located in `test/index.js`. When trying to find out how a feature within a module works, the one-to-one mapping makes it much easier to find the associated tests, and see examples of it in use.

So, having separated our server from our tests, let's look at what our two files now look like; first, `lib/index.js`:

```
const Hapi = require('hapi');
const server = new Hapi.Server();
server.connection();
server.route({
  method: 'GET',
  path: '/',
  handler: function (request, reply) {
    return reply('Hello World\n');
  }
});
module.exports = server;
```

The main change here is that we export our server at the end for another file to require and start it if necessary. Our test file in `test/index.js` will now look like:

```
const Code = require('code');
const Lab = require('lab');
const server = require('../lib/index.js');
const lab = exports.lab = Lab.script();
lab.test('It will return Hello World', (done) => {
  server.inject('/', (res) => {
    Code.expect(res.statusCode).to.equal(200);
    Code.expect(res.result).to.equal('Hello World\n');
    done();
  });
});
```

Finally, for us to test our code coverage, we update our `npm test` script to include the coverage flag, `--coverage` or `-c`. If you run this, you'll find we actually already have 100% of the code covered with this one test. An interesting exercise here would be to find out the versions of hapi that this code functions correctly with. At the time of writing, this code was written for hapi version 11.x.x on Node.js version 4.0.0. Will it work if run against hapi version 9 or 10? You can test this now by installing an older version with:

```
$ npm install hapi@10
```

This will give you an idea of how easy it can be to check whether your codebase works against different versions of libraries. If you have some time, it would be interesting to see how this example runs on the different versions of Node. (Hint: it breaks on any version earlier than 4.0.0!)

In this example, we got 100% code coverage with one test. Unfortunately, we are rarely this lucky. With an increase in the complexity of our codebase, there is an increase in the complexity of our tests, which is where knowledge writing testable code comes in. This is something that comes with practice by writing tests while writing application or module code.

Linting

Also built into lab is linting support. Linting is the process of using static analysis to check if a code style is adhered to. The rules of the code style can be defined by an `.eslintrc` or `.jshintrc` file. By default, lab will enforce the hapi style guide rules mentioned in the first chapter of this book.

The idea of linting is that all code will have the same structure, making it much easier to spot bugs and to keep the code tidy. As JavaScript is a very flexible language, linters are used regularly to forbid bad practices such as global or unused variables.

To enable the lab linter, simply add the linter flag to the test command, which is `--lint` or `-L`. I generally stick with the default hapi style guide rules, as they are chosen to promote easy-to-read code that is easily testable and forbids many bad practices. However, it's easy to customize the linting rules used; for this, I also recommend referring to the `lab` documentation.

Summary

In this chapter, we've looked at testing in Node and hapi, and how testing as well as code coverage are paramount in the hapi ecosystem. We've seen justification for their needs in application development, and how they can make us a more productive developer.

We've also introduced the test runner and code assertion libraries lab and code in the ecosystem and justified their use. You've learnt how to use them for writing simple tests, and how to use the tools provided in lab and hapi to test hapi applications.

You've also learned of some of the extra features baked into lab such as code coverage and linting. We looked at testing the code coverage of an application and getting it to 100%, and explained how the hapi ecosystem applies the hapi style guide to all the modules using the linting integration `inlab`.

As always, all code samples seen here as well as some extra material can be found online in the repository available at `https://github.com/johnbrett/Getting-Started-with-hapi.js`.

However, I highly recommend reading through the code associated with this chapter, especially, as I've also updated the user store example from the previous chapter to include tests with 100% code coverage.

Now that you have learned how to secure your code, and ensure that it does what you expect through testing, we will look at securing our applications through authentication and authorization in the next chapter.

5
Securing Applications with Authentication and Authorization

In this chapter, we're going to explore different methods of securing an application through authentication and authorization. We'll talk about some of the basics of each concept, and then show how hapi simplifies the process of adding both to an application in an easy-to-manage, configurable way.

Fortunately, hapi is a security-focused framework, and as mentioned throughout this book, aims to ensure that developers don't accidentally use the wrong defaults when it comes to implementing things such as security. Therefore, right from the framework's inception, it has had core support for both authentication and authorization, rather than leaving it up to a third-party module. Application security is core to almost every application nowadays; it's not enough for it to be an afterthought in an application or a framework.

When first working with a new technology or framework, security was usually the first stumbling block I arrived at, where either I had to implement my own authentication, which is risky as I'm not a security expert, or I had to use a library which performed some under-the-hood magic which I didn't understand. This meant that I lost the opportunity to learn about the underlying security protocols and implementation. hapi does neither; instead it exposes the tools we need, in an easy-to-use, manageable, and understandable form. Let's look at the way to add authentication and authorization to our applications now, starting with authentication.

Authentication

Authentication is the process of determining whether a user is who they claim to be. For example, for whatever username they supply, they have another determining factor that proves that they are who they say there are. Most often, this is done by supplying a secret that only the user would know, such as a password.

In most applications, this username and password combination will return or create a token that will be stored somewhere with the user, so all future interactions within the application won't need to be re-authenticated with the same username and password. This token is usually stored in a cookie.

In both cases, we would usually take the password, token, or any other form of access key from the request to our application by parsing headers or cookies, depending on the type of authentication, and compare it with some data which is stored in our database. For those of you familiar with authentication, you may recognize the authentication protocols that have been described just now as basic and cookie.

Both these protocols can be described in two stages. The first stage is the acquisition of the token, or the underlying mechanics of the authentication protocol such as parsing the authorization header of a request. In hapi, this is called a scheme. To create an authentication scheme in hapi, you would use the `server.auth.scheme()` API as follows:

```
...
server.auth.scheme('basic', (server, options) => {
  // do token parsing logic here
});
...
```

Fortunately, there are plugins in the hapi ecosystem that cover most types of authentication schemes for you, and register the authentication scheme when you register the plugin. Unless you are writing a new authentication protocol, you will likely never need to write a scheme for your hapi application, but it's good to know what these authentication scheme plugins do under the hood. We'll explore examples demonstrating these plugins in use later in this chapter.

The second stage is where we take our token, or the username and password combination, and compare it with something in our database to check if they are valid. In hapi, this is what we call a strategy. Unlike schemes, your strategies will be application-specific, and will likely be implemented as per application. Strategies are registered using the `server.auth.strategy()` API as follows:

```
...
const validate = function (request, username, password, next) {
  // perform validation logic here
```

```
};
const basicConfiguration = { validateFunc: validate };
server.auth.strategy('simple', 'basic', basicConfiguration);
...
```

There are a few things happening in this preceding example, so let's go through it in more detail. When registering a strategy, we supply the following:

- The name of the strategy we are creating; here it is `simple`.

- The name of the scheme that the strategy will use, which has previously been registered through `server.auth.scheme()`. Here the scheme used is `basic`.

- An object containing the required configuration to validate credentials, which is specific to the scheme. With the `basic` authentication scheme, all that is required is an object with a function called `validateFunc` that validates credentials.

It's worth knowing that we can actually register multiple schemes and strategies within our application. This is very common and is very useful when applying one strategy to the API endpoints, such as a Bearer token or OAuth workflow, and a different strategy for authentication when viewing templates or views within an application, where something like cookie-based authentication would be more suitable.

Following the registering of our strategy, we then have multiple ways of applying a particular authentication strategy to our application. We can apply it through the route configuration object if we need a route-specific authentication, or set the strategy to be applied to all our routes as the default.

This is a lot to take in at once and may still be a little unclear, but it will hopefully become much easier to understand when we go through a few examples using different forms of authentication. We will also look at how to configure authentication strategies globally or to specific routes. Let's look at a few examples of registering some authentication schemes and strategies now. If you want to run any of these examples yourself, all these examples are available in the source code supplied with this book, which can be found in the GitHub repository available at `https://github.com/johnbrett/Getting-Started-with-hapi.js`.

Configuring authentication

Let's look at adding authentication to a server now. The first example will use the basic authentication scheme. Aptly named, the basic authentication scheme is the simplest authentication scheme to use for an app, and is a great place to start when learning about authentication.

The following example shows us the multiple steps of adding an authentication scheme to an application in hapi. First we install the `hapi-auth-basic` plugin (`https://github.com/hapijs/hapi-auth-basic`) from npm:

```
$ npm install hapi-auth-basic --save
```

In our application code, we then require the plugin which, when registered, will register the `basic` scheme. We then add a strategy and apply it to our routes. Let's look at what that looks like now. I've broken this code example into the following two files, so it is easier to digest:

- `index.js`: It contains all the authentication configuration and server logic
- `routes.js`: It contains some route configuration objects

Let's go through what this looks like now:

```javascript
const Hapi = require('hapi');
const Basic = require('hapi-auth-basic');                  // [1]
const Blipp = require('blipp');
const routes = require('./routes');
const server = new Hapi.Server();
server.connection({ port: 1337 });
server.register([
  Basic,                                                   // [2]
   { register: Blipp, options: { showAuth: true } }        // [3]
], (err) => {
    // handler err
    const basicConfig = {
      validateFunc: function (request, username, password,
        callback) {
        if (username !== 'admin' || password !== 'password') {
          return callback(null, false);
        }
        return callback(null, true, { username: 'admin' });
      }
    };
    server.auth.strategy('simple', 'basic', basicConfig); // [4]
    server.auth.default('simple');                          // [5]
    server.route(routes);                                   // [6]
    server.start(() => {});                                 // [7]
});
```

With reference to the numbers in the comments in the preceding code, let's go through the explanation:

- [1]: We require the `hapi-auth-basic` module, and store it in the variable `Basic`.

- [2]: We register `basic`, the authentication scheme.

- [3]: We also register `blipp`, but this time configure it to display authentication information for our routes as well as the routing table.

- [4]: We set our strategy for the `basic` authentication scheme. Here, we specify the name as `simple`; it uses the `basic` authentication scheme, which has been already registered, and pass it the configuration object that the `basic` authentication scheme expects. This configuration object is just an object with the function `validateFunc` that performs the actual validation of credentials when passed from a request. More on that in a bit.

- [5]: We set the `simple` authentication strategy we just registered to be `required` on all routes on our server. This can and will be overwritten in the route-specific configuration when we look at our `routes.js` file.

- [6]: We add our routes.

- [7]: I've just trimmed down our server start for brevity, but always remember to handle errors here; it will save hours of debugging if you ever find yourself with a server not starting without an error!

Hopefully, that was easy enough to follow. Now let's look at the `validateFunc` function of our basic config in more detail. You see this has our `request`, `username`, `password`, and `callback` parameters. While all the other parameters are self-explanatory, the callback here is worth explaining. The callback here is in the form:

```
callback(error, isAuthenticated, credentials)
```

The explanation of these parameters are as follows:

- `error`: There was an error trying to valid the credentials of the user

- `isAuthenticated`: The user was successfully authenticated from the given credentials

- `credentials`: User information; this accepts an object, and will attach any values here to the `request.auth.credentials`, which can be used later in the request life cycle such as in our handlers and route prerequisites

If an error is passed back, it will be treated as most errors in hapi: a `boom` error will be sent as is, whereas an unwrapped `Error` object will result in an internal server error.

If we run this example, we now get the authentication info as well from `blipp`. Let's see what this looks like:

```
bash-3.2$ node index.js
http://Johns-Home-Mac.local:1337
    GET     /private                        simple
    GET     /public                         none

Server running at: http://Johns-Home-Mac.local:1337
```

Straight away, we can see our routes with authentication info applied, but one of our routes has the authentication `simple` applied, while the other doesn't! Let's look at `routes.js` to see why that might be:

```javascript
module.exports = [
  {
    method: 'GET',
    path: '/public',
    config: {
      auth: false,
      handler: function (request, reply) {
        return reply(request.auth);
      }
    }
  },
  {
    method: 'GET',
    path: '/private',
    config: {
      handler: function (request, reply) {
        return reply(request.auth);
      }
    }
  }
];
```

If you look at the public route, there's a new property added inside config object, `auth`, which is set to `false`. This basically registers the route, but applies no authentication strategy to it, which explains why there is no authentication applied to our `/public` route.

Noticing that both routes return the auth information for a request in their reply, try running this example, visiting the /public and /private routes, and taking note of the responses. What you will see if you try accessing the /private route, while unauthenticated, is an HTTP-friendly 404 unauthorized error, via the boom module.

What you saw in the preceding code, with auth set to false on the /public route, was the authentication mode applied to this route. There are actually a number of authentication modes that can be set for a strategy or route, such as the following:

- false: It means no authentication is applied to this route

- required: It means credentials must be present and are valid

- try: It means if credentials are present, attempt a login, but continue with request life cycle even if the attempt fails

- optional: It means if credentials are present, attempt to authenticate; if it fails, the request fails

Authentication modes are quite convenient when it comes to login and logout pages that may or may not have an authentication strategy applied.

There is a major downfall with the basic authentication protocol, which you may have already spotted; for this type of authentication, user credentials are required for every request—one of the reasons why it is rarely used in applications. A much more common approach is to have the user enter credentials once, and then use a cookie to store their credentials for future requests. Let's look at how we would do this now.

Cookie authentication

Probably the most common authentication scheme for websites and web applications is to use cookies for storing user credentials and security tokens. As hapi-auth-basic provides us with the basic authentication scheme, hapi-auth-cookie (https://github.com/hapijs/hapi-auth-cookie) provides us with a cookie-based authentication scheme.

Cookie-based authentication is slightly more complicated than our previous example with basic, as we have to manage sessions. With basic auth, we had to provide credentials with every request. In cookie auth, we set the cookie and then we can visit multiple pages without re-authenticating until that cookie expires.

To deal with this session handling, `hapi-auth-cookie` decorates the `request.auth.session` object with methods to set and clear the cookies. Let's look at an example of `hapi-auth-cookie` in action. Again, we'll split our example into an index file for all the server and authentication logic, and a routes file for all our route configuration. Let's look at what that looks like now. First, `index.js`:

```
const Hapi = require('hapi');
const Cookie = require('hapi-auth-cookie');
const Blipp = require('blipp');
const routes = require('./routes');
const server = new Hapi.Server();
server.connection({ port: 1337 });
server.register([
  Cookie,
  Blipp
], (err) => {
  // handler err
  server.auth.strategy(
    'session',
    'cookie',
    {
      cookie: 'example',
      password: 'secret',
      isSecure: false,
      redirectTo: '/login',
      redirectOnTry: false
    }
  );
  server.auth.default('session');
  server.route(routes);
  server.start(() => {});
});
```

In this example, you'll notice that we don't have a `validateFunc` function in our authentication configuration object. This is because with `hapi-auth-cookie`, it's our responsibility to validate the credentials and then call `request.auth.session.set()` to create a session if that user has been successfully authenticated.

In the authentication scheme configuration object, the properties are as follows:

- `cookie`: This is the name of the cookie.
- `password`: This is used to encrypt the cookie with iron (`https://github.com/hueniverse/iron`).

- `isSecure`: This checks whether the cookie is allowed to be transmitted over insecure connections (you should only set this to false during development).

- `redirectTo`: This is a location to redirect unauthenticated requests to. This is useful for simplifying handler logic, so we don't have to worry about redirects for unauthenticated users.

- `redirectOnTry`: This configures whether to attempt redirecting for requests where route authentication is in the `try` mode. The `try` mode configures a route so that if a cookie doesn't exist, the code proceeds without attempting to authenticate. If one does, it attempts to authenticate the user. We will see how this is used in the next example.

Now that we have our `cookie` authentication scheme and strategy registered, let's apply it to some routes and see what this looks like. This will be in our `routes.js` file:

```
module.exports = [
  {
    method: 'GET',
    path: '/login',
    config: {
      auth: {
        mode: 'try'
      },
      handler: function (request, reply) {
        if (request.auth.isAuthenticated === true) {
          return reply.redirect('/private');
        }
        let loginForm = `
          <form method="post" action="/login">
            Username: <input type="text" name="username" />
            <br>
            Password: <input type="password" name="password" />
            <br>
            <input type="submit" value="Login" />
          </form>
          `;
        if (request.query.login === 'failed') {
          loginForm += `<h3>Previous login attempt failed</h3>`;
        }
        return reply(loginForm);
      }
    }
  },
```

```
    {
      method: 'POST',
      path: '/login',
      config: {
        auth: {
          mode: 'try'
        },
        handler: function (request, reply) {
          if (request.payload.username !== 'admin' ||
            request.payload.password !== 'password') {
            request.auth.session.clear();
            return reply.redirect('/login?login=failed');
          }
          request.auth.session.set({
            username: request.payload.username,
              lastLogin: new Date()
          });
          return reply.redirect('/private');
        }
      }
    },
    {
      method: 'GET',
      path: '/public',
      config: {
        auth: {
          mode: 'try'
        },
        handler: function (request, reply) {
          return reply(request.auth);
        }
      }
    },
    {
      method: 'GET',
      path: '/private',
      config: {
        handler: function (request, reply) {
          return reply(request.auth);
        }
      }
    }
  ];
```

Here we have added four routes as displayed in our blipp output:

```
bash-3.2$ node index.js
http://127.0.0.1:1337
    GET    /login                    session
    POST   /login                    session
    GET    /private                  session
    GET    /public                   session
```

You might have noticed that all routes have the `session` authentication strategy applied to them in this example, although some routes use the `try` mode, I'll explain how that is useful in a bit. First, let's go through what is happening in each route here.

We first have two `/login` routes, one being a GET and one a POST route. The GET `/login` route will return the HTML for our login form, but has some extra logic in there. If the client is already authenticated and tries to access the login route, the authenticated client will be redirected to the `/private` route. This is where the `try` mode is useful; if credentials exist, they will be checked and we can redirect if necessary. If not, we just display the login form. We also check if there has been an unsuccessful authentication attempt, and if so, display a message to the user.

The POST `/login` route is where the actual authentication process takes place. Here we compare the payload parameters against our hardcoded strings. If this fails, we clear any session cookies, and redirect the client back to the login page with the `query` parameter set so that we will show the login failed message mentioned in the GET `/login` route.

Next is the GET `/public` route. This just displays the current authentication information. You should run this code example, and visit the `/public` route once while unauthenticated and once after authenticating to note the differences in the `request.auth` object that is returned. You might be curious why the `try` authentication mode would be used here in the route configuration object. If you think of a website sucha as Amazon, you can view product pages while not signed in, and in the top right of the page you see a message like **Sign in**, but if a cookie exists with the correct credentials, you would see a message like **Hello User**. The `try` authentication mode makes this functionality very easy; if no cookie exists, show the normal page; if one does, authenticate the user and perform any required customizations to the required page.

Finally, we have the GET `/private` route. Unlike the public route, where a client may or may not be authenticated, this route requires the user to be successfully authenticated, or they will be redirected to the login page.

It is worth taking some time here to look in depth at the source code associated with the book for this chapter, and test this example. Try visiting each route while authenticated and unauthenticated. A good exercise to test your knowledge of authentication so far would be to try and add a GET /logout route to this example.

Third-party authentication

It is becoming more and more common in web applications to use a third party, such as Twitter or GitHub, for authentication. Using third parties for authentication means potential users for your application can just use the credentials and profile of an existing service to save them from completing tedious signup forms.

This, much like with the other authentication examples we've seen, are made much easier to implement using a hapi plugin. The plugin for third-party authentication is called bell (https://github.com/hapijs/bell). It is worth noting that bell doesn't support any kind of session management, so it is usually combined with hapi-auth-cookie to form a full authentication solution.

Let's try to build an application now that will use two authentication strategies to form the full authentication flow. We will use bell to authenticate a user with Twitter and then hapi-auth-cookie to maintain the session. Let's see what this looks like, again splitting the application into two files: index.js for the server and authentication logic, and routes.js for our route configuration. Let's look at what our index.js would look like:

```
const Hapi = require('hapi');
const Cookie = require('hapi-auth-cookie');
const Bell = require('bell');
const Blipp = require('blipp');
const routes = require('./routes');
const server = new Hapi.Server();
server.connection({ host: '127.0.0.1', port: 1337 });
server.register([
  Cookie,
  Bell,
  { register: Blipp, options: { showAuth: true } }
], (err) => {
  // handle err logic
  server.auth.strategy(
    'session',
    'cookie',
    {
      cookie: 'example',
      password: 'password',
```

```
      isSecure: false,
      redirectTo: '/login',
      redirectOnTry: false
    }
  );
  // Acquire the clientId and clientSecret by creating a
  // twitter application at https://apps.twitter.com/app/new
  server.auth.strategy(
    'twitter',
    'bell',
    {
      provider: 'twitter',
      password: 'cookie_encryption_password',
      clientId: '',
      clientSecret: '',
      isSecure: false
    }
  );
  server.route(routes);
  server.start(() => {});
});
```

Hopefully, all this looks familiar, except that we have now added in the bell plugin, registered it, and created a second strategy that uses Twitter for authentication with application credentials obtained by creating an application on the Twitter developer site, https://apps.twitter.com/app/new.

Next, let's add some routes to authenticate with Twitter, and store this info in a cookie; this part will be in our route.js file:

```
module.exports = [
  {
    method: 'GET',
    path: '/login',
    config: {
      auth: 'twitter',
      handler: function (request, reply) {
        if (!request.auth.isAuthenticated) {
          request.auth.session.clear();
          return reply('Login failed...');
        }
        request.auth.session.set({
          username: request.auth.credentials.profile.username
        });
```

```
            return reply.redirect('/private');
          }
        }
      },
      {
        method: 'GET',
        path: '/private',
        config: {
          auth: 'session',
          handler: function (request, reply) {
            return reply(request.auth);
          }
        }
      }
    ];
```

Surprisingly, not too much code is required to achieve a session-based login system using a third party this time. Let's go through the function of each route now.

First we have the GET /login route. This route, when going through the authentication stage of the request life cycle, will prompt the client to log in to Twitter. Upon successful authentication, the request.auth.credentials will be populated with the response from the Twitter authentication step. From this, we take the username from the Twitter response, store it in our credentials object for our session and call request.auth.session.set() to create our session, and finally, redirect to our /private route.

Our private route which is only accessible to an authenticated user, is now accessible and displays the authentication details for the request, complete with the client's username. If you delete the cookie and try accessing this route again, you will be redirected to the login route as specified in the cookie authentication strategy configuration object.

As a good exercise to solidify your knowledge of authentication, I recommend trying to implement third-party authentication with a different service provider than Twitter, such as GitHub. The third-party authentication workflow can be difficult to grasp, so I recommend running this example, and going through the twitter workflow at the very least.

Authentication summary

So far in this chapter, we covered the concepts of schemes and strategies that hapi uses to implement authentication. We looked in depth at examples of different authentication workflows such as basic cookie-based session authentication, and using third-party providers for authentication.

We looked at the different authentication modes included with hapi, such as `try`, `optional`, and `required`, the cases where they are useful, configuring them as default or route-specific for a server, and also accessing authentication information and credentials in our route handlers through `request.auth`.

Hopefully, this section has given you a good grasp of how authentication works in hapi, and how its core support and modules, covering most types of authentication, greatly simplify the different types of authentication workflow that your application may need.

In the next section, we will look at authorization in hapi and through hapi scopes, and implementing basic permission systems, a very common feature in most applications.

Authorization

While authentication is a process of verifying the identity of a user, authorization is the process of verifying whether they have the permission to access a resource.

Fortunately, hapi has core support for authorization through scopes that allow us to effectively assign a role to a client when we authenticate them, which may be something such as user or admin.

We can then easily specify what roles are authorized to access a route in our route configuration object through the scope property, by passing a string or array of strings. Let's take a look at what a sample application using scopes would look like:

```
const Hapi = require('hapi');
const Basic = require('hapi-auth-basic');
const server = new Hapi.Server();
server.connection({ port: 1337 });
server.register([
  Basic
], (err) => {
  // handle err logic
  const basicConfig = {
```

```
    validateFunc: function (request, username, password, callback)
    {
      if (username === 'admin1' && password === 'password') {
        return callback(null, true, { user: 'admin1', scope:
          'admin' });
      }
      if (username === 'user2' && password === 'password') {
        return callback(null, true, { user: 'user2', scope:
          'user' });
      }
      return callback(null, false);
    }
  };
  server.auth.strategy('simple', 'basic', basicConfig);
  server.auth.default('simple');
  server.route([
    {
      method: 'GET',
      path: '/admin',
      config: {
        auth: {
          access: {
            scope: ['admin']
          }
        },
        handler: function (request, reply) {
          return reply(request.auth);
        }
      }
    },
    {
      method: 'GET',
      path: '/any',
      config: {
        handler: function (request, reply) {
          return reply(request.auth);
        }
      }
    }
  ]);
  server.start(() => {});
});
```

So this looks quite similar to our first `basic` authentication scheme example, except that you may have noticed that in our `basicConfig` configuration object, we have authentication for two different types of users, an admin user and a normal user, and that we assign a corresponding scope:

```
if (username === 'admin1' && password === 'password') {
    return callback(null, true, { user: 'admin1', scope: 'admin' });
}
```

Also, in our `/admin` route, we have added the following:

```
auth: {
  access: {
    scope: ['admin']
  }
}
```

This specifies that any client attempting to access the `/admin` route must be an authenticated user with a scope of `admin`. If not, an HTTP-friendly 403 forbidden error via the `boom` module will be returned to the client.

In the `scope` array, multiple scopes can be used, which would mean that this route is accessible to a user with any of the following roles, not all of the roles.

The second route, however, doesn't have any scopes configured on the route, and so any authenticated user can access this route, regardless of whether they have a scope.

The scope array actually provides very flexible authorization options, not demonstrated here. For example, if a string in the scope array begins with a +, that scope is required. If a string in the scope array beings with a !, it means that scope is forbidden. You can read more about the available scope options in the API documentation at `http://hapijs.com/api#route-options`.

As mentioned earlier, permission levels are something usually quite common to an application; hapi scopes make for a very easy-to-use and manageable solution for creating an authorization system.

Summary

In this chapter, we've looked at some basic methods of securing an application with hapi using multiple workflows in an easy-to-manage manner, without interfering with our internal application logic.

We looked first at authentication with hapi, and how it employs the concepts of schemes and strategies to simplify our authentication workflows. We looked at the `basic` authentication scheme, mainly to demonstrate how authentication would be configured in hapi. We then looked at the more commonly employed `cookie` authentication scheme, and how it can be used to implement a session for our web applications.

Finally, for authentication, we looked at using third-party services as authentication sources, and combining them with session authentication to maintain state between requests.

Following authentication, we explored hapi's support for authorization, and using scopes to implement simple route-level permissions for our apps.

Hopefully, this chapter has given you a good overview of different methods of securing your hapi application in a sane and structured manner.

In the next chapter, we will look at simplifying validation of both routes and internal logic into reusable models that we can use throughout our applications using the model validation library joi.

6
The joi of Reusable Validation

In this chapter, we're going to look at validation in Node and also at joi, the object schema validator used throughout the hapi framework and its ecosystem.

We have actually already touched on joi in *Chapter 2, Adding Functionality by Routing Requests*, when we saw a then unfamiliar type description on a request parameter in our route configuration example. However, joi isn't limited to validating request properties, or even to use within hapi. It is a standalone object schema validation library that can be used in any Node application. Before we delve into some joi syntax and examples, let's first explore the topic of validation first.

An introduction to validation

In pretty much any type of application, we are going to work with data, and of course, we need to ensure that this data is of a certain type or structure before we can act on it. This poses a number of problems. First, how do we easily define the way we want our data to be structured (often referred to as a schema), and second, how can we provide feedback in a consistent manner if the data provided isn't structured the way we want.

As with testing, if it's not easy to write or understand a schema, often, as developers, we won't do it, and instead, resort to very primitive attempts such as:

```
...
if (typeof username !== 'string') {
  // throw or return error
}
// perform action
...
```

First of all, please note that if you find yourself doing this, you're going to have huge problems as your application logic grows. You might have already seen examples of this — massive validation functions for performing actions with different combinations of properties.

This is hugely counterproductive for a number of reasons. Any developer reading this combination of `if` statements will be none the wiser as to what the expected data should look like, just a list of things that it shouldn't be. Secondly, code like this is hard to maintain. It's hard to read, update, and of course 100% test coverage, the importance of which we looked at in *Chapter 5, Securing Applications with Authentication and Authorization*, is hard to obtain. As a general rule, I find the need for `typeof` to be used in business logic a code smell; it should be reserved for libraries.

In practice, I generally try to have the following structure throughout an application:

- Accept objects instead of using multiple parameters to describe any application, that is, 'configuration over code'.

- Any function that accepts an object as a parameter should have a schema for each object, especially if it's a 'public' function, that is, a function exposed by your module, library and so on. This provides both a safety net and documentation for the next developer.

- Validate all inputs by their schema before interacting with any data. This makes for a separation of concerns that leads to a much clearer code.

With the preceding goals in mind, let's now look at joi, and how we might achieve these goals with it.

Introduction to joi

As mentioned earlier, joi (`https://github.com/hapijs/joi`) is an object schema validation library used in nearly every module throughout the hapi ecosystem. If you tried adding an incorrect configuration object to a connection, a route configuration object, or when registering plugins, and found that the server threw a detailed validation error, that was joi at work. When the hapi team were going for a configuration-over-code approach for building a framework, having an excellent object schema validator to validate all the configuration objects and provide detailed errors was important. The same goes for when building an application.

Similar to testing, validation is one of those things that developers might not give the full effort to in projects, as the repercussions aren't immediately obvious. If it's not made easy, it might not be done properly. Fortunately, joi has such an easy-to-use fluent API, that using method chaining, which I'll show soon, makes it very easy to write validation schemas. This makes for readable schemas that act as good documentation for your code. It's also very flexible in the way you can define schemas, with support for using nested schemas for more complex use cases. Let's look at what a simple schema looks like. Let's create a very simple schema to validate a potential username:

```
const usernameSchema = Joi.string().min(4).max(40);
```

Hopefully, it's pretty easy to gather what the schema validates. Given an input, it checks for a string that has a minimum length of 4 characters and maximum length of 40 characters.

We can then test joi schemas against their inputs using `joi.assert()` or `joi.validate()`. The difference between the two is that `joi.assert()` returns the result or throws an error when it is called, whereas `joi.validate()` always returns an object of the form:

```
{ error: … , value: … }
```

Here `error` will be null if the validation is successful, and `value` will be the resulting object. An optional synchronous callback can be used for dealing with the output of the validation call as well. Let's now try and test our `usernameSchema` parameter with some test cases, and examine the outputs:

```
Joi.validate('john', usernameSchema);
// output:
//   { error: null, value: 'john' }

Joi.validate('jo', usernameSchema);
// output:
//   {    error:
//      { [ValidationError: "value" length must be at least 4
//          characters long]
//        name: 'ValidationError',
//        details: [ [Object] ],
//        _object: 'jo',
//        annotate: [Function] },
//      value: 'jo' }
```

This demonstrates how to validate some simple values pretty easily. A common error I see new users encountering is allowing empty strings. The initial thought might be to just set `joi.string().min(0)`, but this actually won't allow an empty string, as they are not allowed by default. To allow an empty string, we use the following function:

```
Joi.string().allow('');
```

An empty string is a falsey value in JavaScript, so it is better to be secure by default here when allowing empty strings. By using `.allow('')`, you acknowledge that you're allowing potential falsey values. This is a common source of bugs that I notice when something like the following is used:

```
// check is username is defined
if (user.username) {
  // perform some action if username is defined
}
```

Here the username could be defined, but with a falsey value, which means the `if` statement evaluates to `false`. This is something to be conscious of when allowing empty strings or working with other potential falsey values.

The preceding example is still quite trivial, and could easily be replicated with a single `if` statement. Let's now look at a more complex or real-world example where we want to validate a full user object and its properties instead of a simple string.

Given joi's fluent API, to create a schema for an object, we will use `joi.object()` for the schema instead of `joi.string()`. To test the properties within an object, we then use `joi.object().keys({})`. Let's create a user schema now that checks that a given input is an object, with a username property within:

```
const userSchema = Joi.object.keys({
  username: Joi.string().min(4).max(40)
});
```

Again, not too complicated and very readable. We also defined our schema for our username earlier, so we can just reuse that here:

```
const userSchema = Joi.object.keys({
  username: usernameSchema
});
```

This is an example of reusing and nesting schemas. You can nest complete objects within objects, which makes for quite detailed and complex schemas in joi. You can also modify existing schemas through method chaining. Let's demonstrate this by making it such that the username property on our user object is required. This is achieved by adding `.required()` to our existing usernameSchema:

```
const userSchema = Joi.object.keys({
  username: usernameSchema.required()
});
```

Real world cases of these schemas require more logic than just checking whether a key exists or an object property is of a certain type. Often, we will need to rename keys, make it such that two keys can't exist at the same time, or ensure that a minimum number of keys are provided. The good news is that joi supports all these use cases, and I recommend reading its API documentation extensively. Let's add more validations to our userSchema object to demonstrate some of these cases.

When thinking about a potential user schema for an application, usually what we want to record is an identifier such as an e-mail or a username. We'd also want to record a password and then store some extra meta information about our users. Given this, let's add some extra validation rules to our userSchema to allow the email, username, password, and meta keys. Let's also assume that we only want one way to verify a user, either by their email or by their username, so they can't have both. We also want to verify that the e-mail provided is, in fact, a valid e-mail, that the password provided is a string of minimum length 3 and maximum length 30 using only alphanumeric characters, and finally, that our meta will be an object that can store any keys.

 Please note, it is bad security practice to put a maximum length on passwords, or limiting the content to alphanumeric characters. Here, the validation rules we have added are to highlight the flexibility of joi only. If this were a production system, I would likely have only a minimum password length validation rule, and a much higher maximum — in the region of 1024, if at all.

In joi, we could represent this by the following schema:

```
const usernameSchema = Joi.string().min(4).max(40);
const userSchema = Joi.object().keys({
  username: usernameSchema.required(),
  email: Joi.string().email(),
  password: Joi.string().regex(/^[a-zA-Z0-9]{3,30}$/),
  meta: Joi.object()
}).xor('username', 'email');
```

Not too complicated and still very readable. If I haven't convinced you on the importance of joi yet, I recommend you to try replicating the preceding `userSchema` with `if` statements now, keeping in mind that you have to provide a consistent and detailed error for each validation step broken—not so easy, right?

If you test this with `joi.validate()`, by default, it aborts all the validation steps once it hits the first validation error. To get all the errors, you would just add the optional third `options` parameter to the call to `joi.validate()`, which will look like the following:

```
Joi.validate(user, userSchema, { abortEarly: false });
```

Now that we have a good grounding in joi, let's look at how and where we would use joi in our hapi applications.

Validating hapi routes with joi

Now that we have learned about the importance of validation and the flexibility of `joi`, let's look at where we can apply it in our hapi applications. Fortunately, hapi provides first class support for validation on its route configuration objects. We saw this very briefly in *Chapter 2, Adding Functionality by Routing Requests*, both on a route configuration object and where the validation steps take place within the request life cycle.

On a route configuration object, we can provide validation rules through a `validate` object. With this, we can define specific validation rules for the request headers, parameters, query, payload, and also on the response. It might not be immediately obvious why we would validate our response, but we'll look at that further on in the chapter. Let's first look at an example of a route configuration with added validation rules.

Let's take our user store application from the previous chapters, and add some validation. If you remember the GET route, we asked the user to provide a string `userId` to retrieve a user, but in our handler, never actually verified that it existed. Let's fix this now by modifying this particular route configuration to add validation rules for ensuring that the `userId` is a string, it exists, and is of the right length. Let's see what that looks like now (with code removed for brevity):

```
...
server.route({
  method: 'GET',
  path: '/user/{userId}',
  config: {
    validate: {
      headers: true,
```

```
      params: {
        userId: Joi.string().min(4).max(40).required()
      },
      query: false
    },
    handler: function (request, reply) {
      // handler logic
    },
    description: 'Retrieve a user'
  }
});
...
```

So, as you can see, it's not too complicated to add validation to our routes in a very readable manner. Let's look more closely at the validate property that we added:

```
...
validate: {
  headers: true,
  params: {
    userId: Joi.string().min(4).max(40).required()
  },
  query: false
},
...
```

We've added three keys to our verification object, so let's go through each of those and examine what they do. Before explaining each, it's worth noting that for each key that we add to the `validate` object, the following values are supported:

- true: This specifies that any value is allowed.

- false: This specifies that no values are allowed.

- A joi validation object: The provided joi validation object dictates what is allowed here.

- A custom validation function: A function with the signature `function(value, options, next)` can be provided, which will dictate what values are allowed here. However, I've rarely seen this used in practice, as joi usually fulfills the need for any validation we may need to do; nevertheless, it is good to be aware that this option exists.

If validation fails on any of these properties, a `Boom.badRequest()` error will be returned to the client, and the request life cycle will never reach the handler.

Now let's go through each of the properties from the preceding example. First, we have specified validation for headers, indicating that any value is allowed by specifying true. If this is ever set to false for headers, it will cause all valid HTTP requests to fail. Adding headers: true is not required; by not adding a value for the headers property, it defaults to true. I have only added it here, so as to show that we can add validation rules to request headers.

For our params, we've supplied a joi object that specifies that one segment is allowed, which is the userId segment of our params. The rules applied are that the userId segment supplied in the request must be of minimum length 4 and maximum length 40.

By specifying query as false, we also specify that no query parameters are allowed or we reject the request. Note that we don't need to specify anything for the payload here, as a payload is never parsed for the GET routes. In fact, even trying to add validation for a HEAD or a GET route will throw an error as a reminder, just as trying to add a validation rule for a parameter that isn't defined in the route path would.

Let's now look at adding validation for POST route. Previously, we applied no validation, which meant that any type of object could be sent as a potential user object. Let's take our userSchema from the previous section, and apply that to the POST route (again, with code removed for brevity):

```
// Our Schemas
const usernameSchema = Joi.string().min(4).max(40);
const userSchema = Joi.object().keys({
  username: usernameSchema.required(),
  email: Joi.string().email(),
  password: Joi.string().regex(/^[a-zA-Z0-9]{3,30}$/),
  meta: Joi.object()
}).xor('username', 'email');

// Route Configuration
server.route({
  method: 'POST',
  path: '/user',
  config: {
    validate: {
      params: false,
      query: false,
      payload: userSchema
    },
    handler: function (request, reply) {
      // handler logic
```

```
    },
    description: 'Create a user'
  }
});
```

Now with those small additions, we validate all our inputs to the user store in a readable manner. By using `joi.object()`, we have more options in how we'd like to handle our payload here as well. If we want to accept extra values outside of our defined rules, we can add `.unknown()` to our `userSchema`.

Now that we're comfortable validating our route inputs, let's look at how and why we would validate our route responses.

Validating route responses

I mentioned earlier that you can also validate the outputs of a route. This can be a particularly useful tool when building APIs that other services may reply upon, and when you want to ensure that any modifications to your handlers or models don't break an existing contract that you've specified.

We can do this by specifying a joi object as the schema that must be matched in our route configuration object. Of course, this validation step will add some performance overhead, so fortunately, we can also specify the percentage of responses we want validated. We can also specify a fail action, whether to send the response even though it doesn't match our expected schema and log it, or we can send a 500 error, indicating an internal server error event. Let's look at how we would configure all of the preceding options on the GET user route for our user store:

```
...
server.route(
  method: 'GET',
  path: '/user/{userId}',
  config: {
    validate: {
      headers: true,
      params: {
        userId: Joi.string().min(4).max(40).required()
      },
      query: false
    },
    handler: function (request, reply) {
      // handler logic
    },
    response: {
```

```
        schema: Joi.object().keys({
          id: Joi.string().min(4).max(40),
          details123: Joi.object()
        }),
        sample: 100,
        failAction: 'error'
      },
      description: 'Retrieve a user'
      }
    }
  );
  ...
```

Here, we see the new response property added to our route configuration object. Even though this is a type of validation, it's configuration is specified via the response property. It's separated from the input validation so that the `validate` property in the route configuration is for input validation only. Let's quickly go through each option in the response configuration object in this example:

- `schema`: This is the response payload validation rule. In the preceding example, it is a joi object, but like the validation properties for the inputs, it could be any of `true`, `false`, a joi object, or a custom validation function.

- `sample`: The percentage of responses we want to validate. Validating our response payload provides a certain overhead, so we may not want to validate all our responses in a production environment. A good strategy here would be to validate all the responses in a development environment, and a much lower number, if any, in production.

- `failAction`: The action we want to take when a response doesn't meet our validation rules. Our options are `error` or `log`. An `error` value here will mean that "500 Internal server error message" is sent to the client if the validation rules aren't met. A value of `log` here means that if the validation rules aren't met, the response will still be sent, but the response logged. A good strategy here would be to use `error` when in development and `log` when in production.

It's worth knowing that we can also pass an extra `options` object here, which will be passed to joi's `validate` function. Be conscious here though, that any options that require modification of the output will require the `modify` response validation option to be set to `true`. All the response validation options are covered in hapi's API documentation at `http://hapijs.com/api#route-options`.

With that, we should be comfortable with validating our response outputs. Let's look at one of my favorite features of hapi next: using all this route configuration to generate API documentation.

Documentation generation

When I was first investigating Node frameworks for building an API, documentation generation was a hugely important feature that I needed. I was building a public API for a proprietary system at the time. Without good documentation, this, or any API, wouldn't garner much usage as you can probably imagine.

As the initial writing of API documentation is a huge chore, one which I don't enjoy anyway, the even more time consuming task is to constantly try to update documentation to keep it in sync with the latest version of the API. For an API under constant development, this would become a huge time sink, and so drove the need for documentation generation. In most frameworks, this generally comes from requiring annotations, and/or compromising the flexibility of route configuration, which aren't great options.

Fortunately, the configuration-over-code approach of hapi lends itself quite well to being able to generate documentation, as we can generate a full routing table with all the route configuration attached, as we have seen with `blipp`. If you read the `blipp` source code (`https://github.com/danielb2/blipp/blob/master/lib/index.js`), you can see it's not very complicated to read the routing table configuration. Can you imagine what this would be like if it were trying to interpret configuration from code as opposed to configuration?

This means we can now generate a JavaScript or JSON representation of all our routes as well as all the inputs that they accept from our attached validation, apart from any description, tags, or notes attached. There are two widely-used libraries that avail of this approach to turn this representation of our routes into a viewable HTML page generated on each startup of our server. These libraries are `lout`, developed by the hapi team (`https://github.com/hapijs/lout`), and `hapi-swagger` (`https://github.com/glennjones/hapi-swagger`). Both use different strategies to achieve the goal of generating route documentation.

`lout` iterates through the hapi server routing table and creates a JavaScript object, which it passes to a template context (as we saw in *Chapter 2, Adding Functionality by Routing Requests*, when using the `vision` module) to serve a template. This works well, and provides a basic view of your routing table with all its input validation rules.

`hapi-swagger` creates our documentation via the swagger library (http://swagger.io/swagger-ui/). It cleverly uses our route configuration to create a swagger-compliant JSON specification of our routes. It then provides a route with an HTML page that loads the `swagger-ui` JavaScript library, which reads in the JSON specification. Through this, the documentation page is created (which is an interactive sandbox) so that you can test all your API endpoints right from this documentation page. I've found that this is a hugely useful feature to have as part of an API to drive adoption, and it saves countless developer hours updating documentation.

Looking again at our user store API example, let's see what effort is required to make our API self-documenting, based on all the validation we have added in this chapter. For this example, we'll use the `hapi-swagger` library to document our API, as this will then give us a sandbox to test any API functionality we add right from the page. Let's get started.

First we need to install the `hapi-swagger` library. We also need to install the `inert` and `vision` libraries, as we will be serving some static files as well as templates. Let's do that now:

```
$ npm install hapi-swagger inert vision
```

Next, we'll modify the `index.js` file of our user store. We need to `require` the `hapi-swagger`, `inert`, and `vision` modules, then register them as plugins against our server. Let's look at the resulting `index.js` with these modifications applied:

```
'use strict';
const Hapi = require('hapi');
const Blipp = require('blipp');
const HapiLevel = require('hapi-level');
const UserStore = require('./user-store.js');
const HapiSwagger = require('hapi-swagger');
const Inert = require('inert');
const Vision = require('vision');
const server = new Hapi.Server();
server.connection({ port: 1337, host: '127.0.0.1' });
server.register([
  { register: HapiLevel, options: { path: './temp', config: {
    valueEncoding: 'json' } } },
  UserStore,
  Blipp,
  Inert,
  Vision,
  HapiSwagger
], (err) => {
```

```
    // handler err
    server.start((err) => {
      // handler err
      console.log(`Server running at ${server.info.uri}`);
    });
  });
```

It's worth noting the importance of handling errors here. In this example, I omit them for brevity, but if you hadn't handled the error when registering plugins or starting your server for example, and were missing one of hapi-swagger's dependencies such as `inert` or `vision`, the server would just exit without an error, in a hard-to-debug fashion. The lesson to be learned: always handle the errors in your callbacks!

Other than that, there's nothing too drastic here. Now as the `hapi-swagger` documentation specifies, it will only document the routes that have an `api` tag added to the route configuration. So, let's that make that change in our `user-store.js` file as well. This would mean modifying our GET route configuration as follows:

```
server.route([
  {
    method: 'GET',
    path: '/user/{userId}',
    config: {
      validate: { … },
      handler: function (request, reply) { … },
      response: { … },
      description: 'Retrieve a user',
      tags: ['api']          // API Tag added.
    }
  }
]);
```

It would also mean doing the same for our POST route. If we launch our hapi application now, we will see that we have some extra routes added in our `blipp` output as seen in the following screenshot:

```
bash-3.2$ node index.js
http://127.0.0.1:1337
  GET    /docs
  GET    /docs/custom.js
  GET    /docs/swaggerui/{path*}
  GET    /docs/swaggerui/images/throbber.gif
  GET    /documentation
  POST   /user                               Create a user
  GET    /user/{userId}                      Retrieve a user

Server running at http://127.0.0.1:1337
```

These are just routes for serving some of the necessary static content for our generated documentation page. That /documentation page looks interesting, though; let's open that up in a browser, and see what we get:

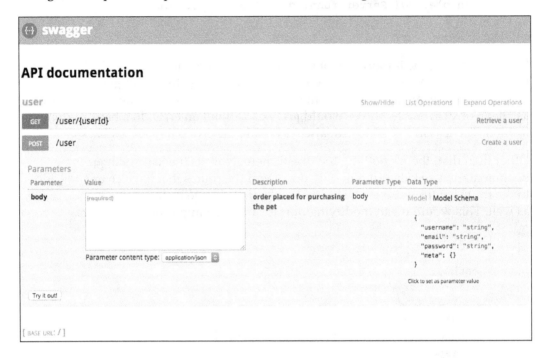

And there we have it—an interactive documentation sandbox with our expected model schema on the right. If you check the GET route documentation, it also lists the expected response schema that we added earlier in the chapter.

For the full range of options in configuring the generated hapi-swagger documentation page, I recommend reading the hapi-swagger repo documentation.

Summary

In this chapter, we've looked at the topic of validation and joi, the object schema validation library used throughout the hapi ecosystem. We looked at the importance of validating our inputs, and how to keep this work manageable by using joi.

Hopefully, this chapter has given you a good grounding in the flexibility of joi, and also in how to make your code more robust and readable so that you can use joi both within or outside of hapi applications. I recommend having a full read of joi's documentation and repo examples before moving on to the next chapter.

One of the drawbacks of joi at the moment is that it only supports server-side validation out of the box. However, as popularity grows, I expect this to change in the future, and with tools such as browserify and webpack, it is possible to use joi in the browser with some work; however, that is outside the scope of this book.

As always, all code samples seen in here as well as some extra material can be found online in the repository available at `https://github.com/johnbrett/Getting-Started-with-hapi.js`.

If you have any questions about the code samples regarding understanding the code snippets or problems running them, feel free to open an issue.

Let's now move on to the final chapter of this book where we will look at some more tools from the hapi ecosystem, which you'll want to cover before we finally get our hapi applications ready for production.

7
Making Your Application Production Ready

So, we're already at the last chapter. I hope you have enjoyed learning about hapi and how to build applications with it so far. In this last chapter, I'd like to cover some of the remaining common tasks that we often encounter when building applications, and getting them ready for production.

Here, you'll learn about the following:

- Using databases to store our data
- Server methods and adding caching to our applications through them
- Logging and the importance of logs for applications in production
- Different tools to add to your tool belt for debugging Node applications as well as some hapi-specific tools from the hapi ecosystem
- Some advice on production infrastructure
- Places you can go to in order to continue your learning about hapi

Let's begin.

Persisting data

I covered persisting data earlier in this book in our user store example using an in-process database called LevelDB. While LevelDB works quite well for demo purposes, due to a very simple installation and setup, it has a very limited feature set, and isn't recognized widely as a production-ready database.

Most applications today use some of the better known and tested databases, such as MongoDB (`https://www.mongodb.org/`), PostgreSQL (`http://www.postgresql.org/`), or MySQL (`https://www.mysql.com/`). While this is because of the wider feature sets that they offer, it is also, as it has been proven in production environments, something of vital importance when it comes to a database. When an application crashes or runs slowly, you'll find you have some frustrated customers, but losing their data usually means you've lost them for good!

Taking this into account, I wanted to add an example to demonstrate integrating one of these databases with hapi to show that this can be done just as easily as we did with our LevelDB example.

Fortunately, for all of the aforementioned databases, there are hapi plugins developed by the community to handle most of the setup of integrating a database with hapi. These, when registered, usually handle the initial connection setup, and will make a database connection available as a property on the request object for our route handlers, or via the `server.plugins['somedatabase']` reference.

The database we'll use for this example is MongoDB, as it is one of the most popular databases as a part of the Node-based technology stack at the moment. MongoDB is a NoSQL document-oriented database if you are not familiar with it. This means that instead of the traditional SQL structured databases such as MySQL or PostgreSQL where data is stored in tables and rows, MongoDB stores data as JSON documents as part of a collection.

NoSQL databases have grown exponentially with the popularity of Node. This is likely down to the fact that they have a smaller learning curve, and data is stored in a format that is easy to interact with from JavaScript. Moreover, they are generally schema-less and meaning less need for big migrations or downtime.

MongoDB

Let's see what is involved in converting our user store example to using MongoDB instead of LevelDB as our database. You'll first need to install MongoDB if you have not done so already. Details on installation for each operating system are provided on the MongoDB website at `https://docs.mongodb.org/manual/`.

While MongoDB has an official driver for Node (`https://www.npmjs.com/package/mongodb`), you'll likely not need to use it directly very often. In Node, most frameworks will have a node module to aid integrating into your application, and hapi here is no different. Here we'll use the `hapi-mongodb` package (`https://www.npmjs.com/package/hapi-mongodb`), which will take care of all the initial setup for integrating a MongoDB connection into our application.

Let's now update our user store example. First we'll start by modifying our application entry point, the index.js file. To use MongoDB instead of LevelDB here actually only requires two changes; I've highlighted both with comments:

```
'use strict';
const Hapi = require('hapi');
const Blipp = require('blipp');
const HapiMongo = require('hapi-mongodb');                    // [1]
const UserStore = require('./user-store.js');
const HapiSwagger = require('hapi-swagger');
const Inert = require('inert');
const Vision = require('vision');
const server = new Hapi.Server();
server.connection({ port: 1337, host: '127.0.0.1' });
server.register([
  { register: HapiMongo, options: { url:
    'mongodb://localhost:27017/user-store' } },               // [2]
  UserStore,
  Blipp,
  Inert,
  Vision,
  HapiSwagger
], (err) => {
  if (err) {
    throw err;
  }
  server.start((err) => {
    if (err) {
      throw err;
    }
    console.log(`Server running at ${server.info.uri}`);
  });
});
```

Let's just explain those comments before moving forward:

- [1]: We require the hapi-mongodb module here instead of where we previously required the hapi-level module
- [2]: We now register the hapi-mongodb module as a plugin in our server

However, if you try run this now (with MongoDB running), you'll find that we get an error:

```
Error: Plugin user-store missing dependency hapi-level in
connection: http://127.0.0.1:1337
```

Can you hazard a guess as to why we get this error? Remember, we declared a dependency on the `hapi-level` plugin back in our original user-store example? Well, this is no longer going to be met; we'll have to update our `user-store.js` file to account for this. We only catch this by handling the error passed to us from the `server.start()` method.

I'd like to highlight the importance of error handling here on the plugin registration also. Without this, our server would start even if MongoDB wasn't running. It's worth testing this; try stopping your MongoDB instance from running and then launching this example again. You should get the following error:

```
Error: connect ECONNREFUSED 127.0.0.1:27017
```

The lesson to be learned here is that you should always handle errors from the start. It'll make you far more productive down the line when things are failing unexpectedly, with no errors being thrown or logged.

Now that we're more comfortable with our error handling, let's finish off updating this example to use MongoDB. There's little more work required to update our `user-store.js` file to use MongoDB than in the `index.js` file. We have to first modify our dependency, then update the logic of how we add and retrieve users to match the MongoDB driver APIs instead of those of LevelDB.

Let's now look at what changes need be made to our `user-store.js` file. As the file itself is quite long, I will just go through the parts that need to be updated, starting with the changes in registering `server.dependency()`:

```
...
let store;
let ObjectID;
server.dependency('hapi-mongodb, (_server, after) => {
  store = _server.plugins['hapi-mongodb'].db.collection('users');
  ObjectID = _server.plugins['hapi-mongodb'].ObjectID;
  return after();
});
...
```

Here we register the variables for `store` and `ObjectID` to use throughout the plugin, which will be updated within the `server.dependency()` callback. You'll notice that I used `_server` here as the variable name. This is not to conflict with the variable server in the outer scope.

The `ObjectID` variable used here is a new concept used in MongoDB, so let me just explain it before moving forward. In LevelDB, we generated our unique identifiers for users via the `uuid` module. MongoDB has its own means of generating IDs, via `ObjectID`, so we will use that here.

Finally, we update the dependency to be on the `hapi-mongodb` plugin as opposed to the `hapi-level` plugin.

Let's now look at the `createUser` and `getUser` functions, as their logic will change slightly to use the MongoDB APIs instead of LevelDBs. Let's look first at the `createUser` function:

```
...
const createUser = function (userDetails, callback) {
  const userId = new ObjectID();
  const user = {
    _id: userId,
    details: userDetails
  };
  store.insertOne(user, (err, result) => {
    if (err) {
      callback(Boom.internal(err));
    }
    getUser(userId, callback);
  });
};
...
```

Here we see the call to `ObjectID()` to create our user ID. It's worth noting the `_id` property used here. MongoDB's `insertOne()` API takes a single object and a callback as opposed to LevelDB's `put()` where we supplied the unique identifier key, user object, and callback. In MongoDB, this identifier key is, instead, placed within the object as the `_id` property, and we'll see how it retrieves a user with it in the `getUser` function. Apart from this change in ID logic, the rest of the function logic remains the same.

Let's now look at our `getUser` function. Previously, this was just one line, but to maintain the same API so that our handler code doesn't need to change, we have to add a little more logic here. Let's see what that looks like:

```
...
const getUser = function (userId, callback) {
  store.findOne({ '_id' : ObjectID(userId) }, (err, result) => {
    if (!result) {
      return callback(Boom.notFound());
    }
    result.id = result._id;
    delete result._id;
    return callback(null, result);
  });
};
...
```

As there're a few changes here, let's go through them in a little more detail.

We are now using Mongo's `findOne()` API as opposed to LevelDB's `get()`. As seen in the `createUser` function, this takes an object with the `_id` property instead of just a string as the identifier key.

The other difference is that LevelDB returns an error when an object was not found by its unique identifier. However, in MongoDB this is actually specified by the `result` variable of the `findOne()` callback being `null`. This means that we have to check for this, and return a `Boom.notFound()` error when `result` is `null`. Next we modify the stored object, so it is structured as our previous response was by removing the `_id` property from our object and adding the `id` property instead.

And that's it! Since we maintained all the same function signature and responses for `createUser` and `getUser` as before, we don't have to update our handler logic for either route. The full code for this example can be found in the examples for this chapter in the *Getting Started with hapi.js* repository on GitHub available at `https://github.com/johnbrett/Getting-Started-with-hapi.js`.

The 'M' in MVC

The previous section covered running basic queries against a database. While this is an easy way to persist and retrieve data from your chosen database, often, as the size of your application grows, so will the number of ways you interact with all this data. To manage this, often the best approach is to build an abstraction layer which handles all of these data queries. This is often referred to as the 'Model' in the very common **Model View Controller** (**MVC**)application design pattern.

If you are planning on building a Node application for the first time, I suggest you try following the MVC pattern initially, as it will aid greatly in trying to structure your application and keeping it manageable. It is probably the most well known design pattern in software development, and you'll find many tutorials on it with a quick Google search.

Often, when working with this 'Model' layer, libraries called ORMs are used. **ORM** stands for **Object Relational Mapper**. These ORM libraries usually offer a way to define a schema for what your data should look like, and then provide methods for storing, retrieving, and updating your data, which means that you can spend more time focusing on your business logic and functionality. There is a downside to ORMs in that they usually only account for the general use cases, and it can get very complex when trying to do something more complicated, or when trying to retrofit one to an existing application. If you want to investigate ORMs more, Mongoose is a very popular ORM for MongoDB (`http://mongoosejs.com/`). Hopefully, this has given you a good background in adding different databases to a hapi application.

Introducing caching

In the previous section, we talked about databases and wiring one up to our user store example. However, in applications, a database will often be the main performance bottleneck in the technology stack. The queries we used in the previous section were quite simple, but as an application grows, so does the complexity of a typical database query. Query complexity, as well as a database growing in size will increase the length of time it takes for a single query to run, making for a poor experience for users of our application.

The best strategy for tackling this is to introduce caching. Fortunately, hapi actually has built-in support for server-side caching through the `catbox` module. `catbox` is a key-value-based object store which has extensions for different storage engines via adapters, such as an in-memory adapter (added by default when we create a server), Redis, and memcached.

As this is quite an advanced part of application development, I won't go into too much detail here, but would like to just make you aware of the support that hapi provides for it. Caching in hapi is provided by a low-level client and a higher level policy, but in reality, you will likely never need to use either, as hapi's server methods provide a great abstraction for adding caching to the existing functionality. Let's take a quick look at server methods first, and then we can look at using them to add some caching to our applications.

Server methods

Server methods are functions you attach to the server, which are available everywhere you have a reference to your server object. These, like plugins, are easy to use and very useful for sharing functionality throughout your applications, and as I mentioned, make it very easy to add caching. Let's take a look at an example of how to register a server method, and use it now.

To demonstrate server methods, let's see what a simple function for returning a hello message and registering it as a server method looks like:

```
const getHello = function (name, next) {
  return next(null, `hello ${name} on ${new Date()}`);
};
server.method('getHello', getHello);
```

So that's not too difficult; just be conscious that the callback to a server method has the following signature:

```
next(err, value)
```

The importance of this is that if we return the value as the first parameter, we are in fact returning an error instead of the value. When it comes to later parts such as caching, errors won't be cached, and you might be left wondering why your caching isn't working.

In the preceding example, we've created a server method that, when called, will return the hello message to a name, along with the current date. We can then call this anywhere we have a reference to the server object with, as follows:

```
server.methods.getHello('world', (err, message) => {
  console.log(message); // prints 'hello world' with date
});
```

Note that if the name used to register contains a . character, the method will be registered as a nested object. This can be useful in sandboxing methods. Consider the following example, noting the . between get and hello:

```
...
server.method('get.hello', getHello);
...
```

This would then actually be called by:

```
server.methods.get.hello('world', (err, message) => {
  console.log(message); // prints 'hello world' with date
});
```

This covers the basics of server methods and the most general of their use cases; if you want to learn more, you can read about them in the API documentation at http://hapijs.com/api#servermethodname-method-options.

Caching with server methods

Now that you've seen server methods, let's use them to add some caching to an application. For this example, we will use the default in-memory adapter. Conveniently, this is created by default for us when we create our hapi server.

Modifying the getHello function from the previous example, this time when we create our server method, we'll add the extra server method options object with some cache configuration:

```
...
server.method('getHello', getHello, {
  cache: {
    expiresIn: 30 * 1000,
```

```
      generateTimeout: 10
    }
  });
  ...
```

We now have a cache built for the getHello server method by providing a configuration object with our cache information. expiresIn specifies how long this response will live for in the cache in milliseconds; in this case, it will cache the getHello response for 30 seconds. generateTimeout here specifies how long it should take for the server method to generate the response before sending a timeout error back to the client that initiated the request. This would obviously need to be increased if we were doing anything more complicated than simply returning a string.

Let's see how we could use this in a route handler now:

```
  ...
  server.route({
    path: '/hello/{name}',
    method: 'GET',
    handler: function (request, reply) {
      const name = request.params.name;
      return server.methods.getHello(name, reply);
    }
  });
  ...
```

Here we call the server method and pass the reply as the server method callback, which means not too much extra complexity has been added to the route handler in order to add an in-memory server-side cache here.

The huge advantage of this is now that if an in-memory cache wasn't suitable for your needs, you could add a different default cache engine using some of the other catbox adapters, and you wouldn't need to update any server methods or route handler code.

It's worth noting here that in order to test or use your cache, unlike earlier where we could test with server.inject(), you must have started your server or at least called server.initialize(). This can be a common source of frustration when adding or testing the cache functionality.

Let's now look at a more real-world example. Let's modify our user store example so that for the GET route where we retrieve a user from the database, it will now cache this in memory so that all future requests for the same user will be retrieved from the cache instead of querying the database every time.

As we saw with the previous example, adding the caching functionality doesn't look too complicated. Here, we will register a server method with cache configuration for the `getUser` function, then update our route handler to call the server method instead of the `getUser` function directly. Let's look at what this looks like now. First, we will add the server method for the `getUser` function:

```
...
server.method('getUser', getUser, {
  cache: {
    expiresIn: 30 * 1000,
    generateTimeout: 1000
  }
});
...
```

Next we make the update to the GET route handler for calling our new server method:

```
...
handler: function (request, reply) {
  const userId = request.params.userId;
  server.methods.getUser(userId, (err, user) => {
    if (!user) {
      return reply(Boom.notFound());
    }
    return reply(user);
  });
},
...
```

So, as we saw with the previous example, it's not very difficult to add some simple caching to our applications, even for more real-world examples. The complete example can be found in the examples for this chapter in the *Getting Started with hapi. js* repository on GitHub (`https://github.com/johnbrett/Getting-Started-with-hapi.js`). I encourage you to run this one and test it out, as I've added some `console.log()` messages to the example to show which requests actually hit the database and which are returned just from the in-memory cache.

While this example is much closer to how caching would be used in the real world, there are still some problems that are left unsolved. If you think about adding UPDATE or DELETE routes to this user store API, you would need methods to invalidate the cache for a user. Without those, we would return out-of-date content for the duration for which the response was in the cache.

For this, we use the `drop()` method that is added when we create a server method. In a sample UPDATE or DELETE route handler, this would work something like the following:

```
...
handler: function (request, reply) {
  const userId = request.params.userId;
  // perform update or delete logic
  server.methods.getUser.cache.drop(userId, () => {
    console.log('user removed from cache ... ');
    return reply({ message: 'user removed from cache!' });
  });
},
...
```

Cache invalidation can actually become a very complex topic in applications, as there is no silver-bullet solution that can be used for every application. While my goal was not to cover caching completely here, as it is quite a large topic on its own, I hope I have given you enough to think about here so that when you build your applications, you'll have a good starting point for adding a layer of server-side caching with hapi.

Introducing logging

"We're a logging company that just happen to stream video"

- A member of the Netflix team

I was once attending a technical talk when I heard the preceding quote. We're all familiar with Netflix, the streaming service, but to a member of their team, they consider themselves a logging company that just serves video. I think this is a great way of highlighting the importance of logs.

If you're planning on running any application in a production environment, having quality logging is absolutely paramount, as it will be one of your only means of visibility into what is happening in the production environment, or of went wrong if you find a server crashing without explanation. If you've ever had to diagnose a production issue before, you'll exactly understand the importance of having quality logs.

There are some criteria that a good logging system should have; for one, logs must be time-stamped and readable for both us humans and for machines. There is also so much we can ascertain by looking directly at logs — this is where machine-readable logs come in, as you'll need the ability to analyze and get statistics on the occurrences of particular events.

Moreover, a good logging system will provide easy access to your logs. Really, they should not be stored on the server in which an application is running. If that server somehow goes up in smoke, so do your precious logs.

hapi has some core support for logs, with the `server.log()` and `request.log()` APIs, but I rarely see these used, as hapi's logging is mainly done through the `good` module (`https://github.com/hapijs/good`).

The module `good` is described as a process monitor rather than a logging tool, which is a better description. It works by listening to events from a hapi application, and then pushes those events to external reporters configured within the application. Some example reports officially maintained by the hapi team are as follows:

- `good-udp`: It broadcasts events to a remote endpoint via udp
- `good-file`: It writes events to a file on the local filesystem
- `good-http`: It broadcasts events to a remote endpoint via a POST request
- `good-console`: It writes events to the local console

There are also some reporters created by the community, some of which push to third-party log management services. You can find a list of these on the `good` repository, *README*.

Let's now look at integrating `good` to set up some logging for an application. Let's just create an `index.js` file, and add the following:

```
const Hapi = require('hapi');
const Good = require('good');
const server = new Hapi.Server();
server.connection({ port: 1337, host: '127.0.0.1' });
server.route({
  path: '/',
  method: 'GET',
  handler: function (request, reply) {
    return reply({ message: 'test' });
  }
});

const goodOptions = {
  opsInterval: 3000,
```

```
    reporters: [
      {
        reporter: require('good-console'),
        events: { ops: '*', response: '*', error: '*' }
      }
    ]
  };

  server.register({ register: Good, options: goodOptions }, (err) => {

    if (err) {
      throw err;
    }

    server.start((err) => {
      server.log(['start'], 'Server started');
      console.log(`Server running at ${server.info.uri}`);
    });
  });
```

Hopefully, by now you're familiar with this setup of requiring and registering a plugin against our hapi server. This time, we register the good module with some extra configuration in which we configure the good-console reporter to report on the following event types:

- ops: This is operational data such as RAM and CPU usage. This logs every 3 seconds as specified by the opsInterval setting.

- response: This is information relating to the request and response received by the server.

- error: This logs information for any requests that return an internal server.

The string following each event type is a filter. Any strings passed in here will filter what is logged by that tag. A value of * indicates that no filter is to be applied. If you launch that application, you will find that a host of useful information is now being logged to the console between the operational and request data, as shown in the following screenshot:

```
Server running at http://127.0.0.1:1337
151216/231131.029, [ops], memory: 39Mb, uptime (seconds): 3.73, load: 1.75341796875,2.02197265625,2.24755859375
151216/231134.032, [ops], memory: 39Mb, uptime (seconds): 6.735, load: 1.77294921875,2.021484375,2.24609375
151216/231137.032, [ops], memory: 39Mb, uptime (seconds): 9.735, load: 1.77294921875,2.021484375,2.24609375
151216/231137.579, [response], http://127.0.0.1:1337: get / {} 200 (36ms)
151216/231140.034, [ops], memory: 40Mb, uptime (seconds): 12.737, load: 2.271484375,2.12060546875,2.27978515625
151216/231143.041, [ops], memory: 40Mb, uptime (seconds): 15.743, load: 2.32958984375,2.134765625,2.28369140625
151216/231144.361, [response], http://127.0.0.1:1337: get / {"test":"value"} 200 (8ms)
151216/231146.042, [ops], memory: 40Mb, uptime (seconds): 18.745, load: 2.32958984375,2.134765625,2.28369140625
```

I will leave it as an exercise for you to modify this example so that it throws an error. This way, you can view the detailed logging information for when it happens. I would also recommend trying to add some file logging using `good-file` as a worthwhile exercise.

Debugging applications

Now that we've prepared ourselves for being able to diagnose issues in production, let's also see the tools available in the Node and hapi ecosystem for debugging applications in our development environment.

Coming from a PHP background which had quite a mature debugger, I always found debugging Node applications a bit more difficult to debug due to JavaScript's asynchronous nature. Fortunately, development tooling is improving around this, with more and more development environments being shipped with integrated Node debugging tools. Let's take a quick look at some of the currently available tools as well as some of the hapi-specific tools for debugging your hapi applications.

The console

This is generally every JavaScript developer's go-to when they have an issue. While it works for smaller issues, I wouldn't recommend trying to use this for everything. When it comes to more complex issues, you will want to have some experience with the node debugger.

The Node debugger

I generally try to make this my go-to tool when debugging applications, as being skilled in debugging an application will make you a productive developer overall. As I mentioned earlier, many IDEs and code editors are coming with an in-built Node debugger, such as Microsoft's open-sourced Visual Studio Code editor (`https://code.visualstudio.com/`), or Webstorm (`https://www.jetbrains.com/webstorm/`) by JetBrains.

At the time of writing this book, I have started doing all my code editing through the Visual Studio Code editor due to its built-in debugger support. These debuggers let you create break points, or use the `debugger` keyword to stop the process at the current location so that you can step through the code, looking at all the variables in the scope, which makes it much easier to diagnose any problems or unexpected behavior you might have encountered.

The debug mode in hapi

When creating a server, adding the following:

```
const server = new Hapi.Server({ debug: { log: ['error'] } });
```

will configure the server to log a detailed stack trace to the console for any routes that return an internal server error 500 response. As specified in the hapi API documentation, this should only be used in a development environment; it's not intended for production.

Profiling heapdumps

Embracing the silly naming conventions of hapi modules is the poop (https://github.com/hapijs/poop) module. Despite the name, this can be a very useful module for diagnosing a crashing process. When registered to a hapi server, for any uncaught exceptions, poop will generate a process .heapsnapshot file, which we can later profile.

This can be useful for identifying things such as what memory was used and where within the application at the time of crash. However, these .heapsnapshot files are a science in themselves. I would recommend reading up on some tutorials like the following when trying to grasp the contents of a heapdump file:

http://addyosmani.com/blog/taming-the-unicorn-easing-javascript-memory-profiling-in-devtools/.

TV

TV (https://github.com/hapijs/tv) is an interactive debug console that can be used with hapi applications. It provides a simple web page for viewing all your server logs. Details on how to use TV can be found on the repo's *README* page.

Debugging summary

Debugging applications has been identified as an area of difficulty in Node, and I expect the tools available for debugging both development and production issues will increase over the coming year, as Node is increasingly adopted in enterprises.

My recommendation for the tools listed here is to be comfortable with all of them before you ever put an application near production. You don't want to discover that your logging was insufficient, or learn to profile your first heapdump in the middle of some downtime. Trust me!

General production advice

From time to time, I see the question of production setups being asked in GitHub issues as well as in some of the hapi community chat rooms, so I thought I would provide some information here. While Eran published a GitHub gist detailing Walmart's setup (`https://gist.github.com/hueniverse/7686452`), they were using hapi mainly as a proxy, and I'm pretty sure most production environments won't be at Walmart's scale dealing with events such as Black Friday.

The production setup I see most often with Node, and one that I have used regularly in my own setups, is to have a dedicated web server such as Nginx or Apache to act as the public interface responding to requests on port 80 for HTTP and 443 for HTTPS. I then use these as a reverse proxy to my Node application running hapi. This is so that HTTPS can be handled by the web server terminated prior to reaching the Node hapi-based application, so the Node applications can focus purely on business logic. Often, I have multiple applications running on a single server, and by using something like Apache, I can use vhost-based proxying to different applications at the web server level.

For managing my node processes, I normally use the Node process monitor PM2 (`https://github.com/Unitech/pm2`), where any deployment tool will run a post-deployment hook for restarting all Node processes, with zero downtime via PM2 and Node's cluster module. It might be tempting to use the *watch & restart* functionality of PM2 here, but don't. That is for development environments. As soon as PM2 is notified of a file change, it will begin to restart the process; this may complete before all the files have been transferred to the production server, creating very unexpected results!

For monitoring and logging, I have used a combination of the module good and third-party services such as New Relic (`http://newrelic.com/`), which have both served well. My main advice here is that whatever you use as your monitoring service is fine, just make you sure you have a monitoring system; you'll figure out your needs pretty quickly. Until then, you're operating in the dark.

For databases, it depends on the application. In some cases, I have just used a database installed on the same server as the hapi application, while in others that required a higher level of security and robustness, I used a separate database server.

Further learning

Congratulations on getting this far! I won't be covering any new topics in hapi in this book, but hopefully, I've convinced you on hapi as a great choice for your next project or for integrating with a current one. I just wanted to take some time before finishing up to point out some places where you can further your learning on hapi.

Getting started with hapi.js GitHub repo

The first place I would turn to learn more about hapi is the code repository associated with this book. As mentioned in each chapter, all code examples associated with the book are located in a GitHub repository at `https://github.com/johnbrett/Getting-Started-with-hapi.js`. If you find that any examples were tough to grasp, or would like to explore them in more detail, I recommend cloning the repository and running each example while taking a look at the code. Trying to expand on any of the code examples will be your best source of learning hapi, Node, or coding in general. If you have any further questions on any of the code or would like to have anything cleared up, I encourage you to open an issue.

I will also add extra sample applications to this repository from time to time, which will cover bigger use cases than those covered in this book. I will also gladly take any requests for any applications you would like to see built in hapi through issues on this repo.

Hapijs.com

The hapi website (`http://hapijs.com`) is a great source of learning material. It contains tutorials that introduce a lot of the basic concepts of hapi, from authentication right down to validation and views. It also has a resources page that contains some sample apps, boilerplate apps, and links to books and videos. It also contains the API documentation from every version of hapi, which is always kept up to date. I really recommend reading the API documentation from start to finish; it may seem like a daunting task, but you'll get through it pretty quickly, trust me. I've done it many times at this stage for each new version of hapi. There is a **Need Help?** page there for signing up to the mentor program if you would like an advisor in hapi, and finally if you're feeling up to the task of trying to contribute to the hapi ecosystem, the **contribute** page has a list of issues tagged with new contributor. I highly recommend trying to get involved in trying to contribute to hapi, the community is amazing and will help you through, and it has been one of the biggest resources for learning and furthering my career in recent years, which of course led me to writing this book!

Makemehapi

Makemehapi is a nodeschool workshopper. If you're unfamiliar with the nodeschool format, it consists of a small self-guided workshop that you install through the command line, and then work through the different steps to complete the workshop. You can do these in your own time, or through the many nodeschool chapters around the world where volunteers like myself will help you through the workshops and answer any questions that you have. You can find all the nodeschool workshops on the nodeschool website at `http://nodeschool.io/`. If you're ever in Ireland, you should drop into the Dublin chapter, and you might find me there!

I highly recommend the makemehapi workshopper to work through some practical examples with hapi. You can install it via the terminal using (one of the only times I'd use a global install!) the following command:

```
$ npm i makemehapi -g
```

Run it with the following command:

```
$ makemehapi
```

Now follow the instructions. If you have any problems, open an issue on the makemehapi repo at `https://github.com/hapijs/makemehapi`. Nodeschool also has a wide variety of courses if you would like to learn more about Node (`https://github.com/workshopper/learnyounode`) or npm (`https://github.com/npm/how-to-npm`).

The hapi community

hapi's community is one of its best assets. I have always found it hugely welcoming to developers of all backgrounds. If you want to ask a question or interact with the hapi community directly, it is highly encouraged, and there are multitude of mediums to do so.

The hapi discussion repo

The first place I would begin is the hapi discussion repo on GitHub available at `https://github.com/hapijs/discuss`

This repo is more for discussion and focuses on questions and answers, as opposed to the main hapi repo where you would raise an issue if you encountered a bug (`https://github.com/hapijs/hapi`). If you read back through closed issues, you'll find many examples of hapi users asking questions to help them debug their problems, and the community helping them out.

Stack Overflow

Stack Overflow has been the main go-to for developers seeking help for as long as I've been a developer! However, as the GitHub community is so strong with hapi, I find questions often get answered quicker and in greater detail there than on Stack Overflow, so you might not find as many examples there as with other frameworks.

hapi Gitter channel

There is a good community (including me!) that will help you out on the hapi Gitter channel (`https://gitter.im/hapijs/hapi`) if you prefer to chat with other hapi users instead of through GitHub issues. You'll still need a GitHub account to use it, but it's free, quite easy to use, and a nice format for discussion.

@hapijs on Twitter

If you work on or are interested in hapi, it's definitely worth following the `@hapijs` twitter account. It is a good place to reach out if you're having trouble, or just want to a have a general chat about hapi. Lots of blogs or hapi-related content are tweeted to and from this account, so if you happen across any good blog posts or books (like this one!), it's a good idea to tweet it to the `@hapijs` account, to publicize it to all the `@hapijs` followers.

Read the code!

The final recommendation I would make is to read the source code. The hapi codebase is one of the best I've ever encountered. Reading it has hugely improved my knowledge of how to structure large-scale codebases. However, I find it quite tough to just have a general read of a codebase and pick up much. A better strategy would be to see how something might be implemented in the framework when using a particular feature such as adding a route.

A good tip for trying to walk through a codebase is to look for the `main` property in the project or the module `package.json`. The main field indicates the primary entry point to the application or module. You should also add this to any module that you create.

Summary

Congratulations on finishing this book! I hope it has given you a huge amount to think about, and furthered your knowledge of hapi greatly so you can start writing robust and fully-featured applications today.

If you're new to Node, moving on from reading examples and working through pre-defined problems to writing your own applications from scratch can be tough. Don't be disheartened if this is the case — this will come with time as you write more. Moreover, in the previous section I've listed plenty of resources to help you along the way.

In this book, we've covered hapi, the configuration-centric framework that helps rapidly build robust APIs and web applications. We've looked at adding functionality to our applications through adding routes and serving different types of content such as JSON, static files, or rendered templates. We then looked at different methods for structuring applications, using hapi's excellent plugin system. Following that, we explored the different options available for securing your application with authentication and authorization, and then test it with hapi's test runner lab. Rounding off our learning of hapi, we looked at hapi's excellent validation library joi, and explained how to use it in your applications for validating general objects, for validating route inputs and outputs, and to generate interactive documentation.

In this chapter, we looked at some of the different aspects common to building applications such as adding production-ready databases, adding caching, the importance of logging and some common logging approaches with hapi, some general production advice, and some places you can visit to continue your learning of hapi, Node, and building applications in general.

Finally, I would just like to again congratulate you on taking your first step towards building applications in hapi, and taking the time to read this book. I'd also like to thank Eran Hammer and the hapi team for creating such a great framework. I hope to see you pop up in the community from time to time, and possibly contribute to it one day.

Index

A

application
  composing from plugins 57-60
  structuring 44
arrow function
  reference link 4
authentication
  configuring 81-85
  cookie authentication 85-89
  defining 80-93
  third-party authentication 90-92
authorization
  defining 93-95

B

Behavior-driven Development (BDD) 73
Blipp
  reference link 22

C

caching
  about 119
  server methods 119, 120
  with server methods 120-123
code coverage 63
code testing
  benefits 64-66
  importance 64-66
command line interface (CLI) 67

D

debugging applications
  about 126
  console 126
  debug mode, in hapi 127
  defining 127
  heapdumps, profiling 127
  node debugger 126
  TV 127
documentation generation
  defining 107-110

F

functionality
  encapsulating, within plugins 45, 46

G

general production advice
  defining 128
glue
  reference link 57

H

hapi (hapi.js)
  about 1, 79
  configuration 16
  installing 11
  learning 2-5
  reference 81
  reference link, for blog 1

logging
  defining 123-125
Loopback
  URL 6
lout
  about 107
  URL 107

M

makemehapi
  defining 130
  URL 130
MongoDB
  URL 114
Mongoose
  URL 118
MySQL
  URL 114

N

Node
  about 2
  URL 130
Node API documentation
  URL 4
Node.js
  about 2
  advantages 2
  URL 2
npm
  URL 2, 130
npm scripts
  reference link 68

P

path matching order
  reference link 25
persisting data
  defining 113, 114
  MongoDB 114-118
plugins
  applications, composing from 57-59
  combining 51-55

consuming 48
dependencies, managing 48, 49
exposing 48
sandboxed functionality, exposing 50
plugins, for authentication
  bell plugin 56
  hapi-auth-basic plugin 55
  hapi-auth-cookie plugin 56
plugins, for logging
  blipp 56
  good 56
plugins, hapi universe
  bassmaste 57
  h2o2 57
  inert 56
  nes 56
  tv 57
  vision 56
poop
  URL 127
PostgreSQL
  URL 114

R

Rails
  URL 6
regression 66
reply interface
  about 31, 32
  custom handlers 33
route configuration
  about 20, 21
  cache 24
  description 22
  handler 23
  method 21
  path 21, 22
  pre 22, 23
  summary 24
  validate 22
route responses
  references 106
  validating 105, 106

S

sandboxed functionality
  exposing 50
SemVer
  URL 9
server methods
  references 120
server routing 20
shot module
  reference link 74
static files
  serving, with inert 34-36
swagger library
  URL 108

T

templates
  serving, with vision 37, 38
Test-driven Development (TDD) 73
testing utilities, hapi ecosystem
  about 67
  approaches 73
  code, installing 67-69
  first test script 70-73
  lab, installing 67-69
Travis CI
  reference link 75

V

validation
  defining 97, 98
vision
  reference link 37
  summary 40
  templates, serving with 37, 38
vision configuration
  about 39
  compileMode 40
  engines 39
  paths 39
Visual Studio Code editor
  URL 126

W

Webstorm
  URL 126

Z

Zepto.js
  URL 6

www.ingramcontent.com/pod-product-compliance
Lightning Source LLC
Chambersburg PA
CBHW060145060326
40690CB00018B/3985